METANOIA

Brother John of Taizé

METANOIA

The Shape of the Christian Life

CASCADE *Books* · Eugene, Oregon

METANOIA
The Shape of the Christian Life

Published in French by Ateliers et Presses de Taizé, 2021 under the title *Metanoia. La grammaire de la vie chrétienne*

Cascade Books
An Imprint of Wipf and Stock Publishers
199 W. 8th Ave., Suite 3
Eugene, OR 97401

www.wipfandstock.com

PAPERBACK ISBN: 978-1-7252-9795-1
HARDCOVER ISBN: 978-1-7252-9796-8
EBOOK ISBN: 978-1-7252-9797-5

Cataloguing-in-Publication data:

Names: Brother John of Taize, author.

Title: Metanoia : the shape of the Christian life / Brother John of Taize.

Description: Eugene, OR: Cascade Books, 2021 | Includes bibliographical references.

Identifiers: ISBN 978-1-7252-9795-1 (paperback) | ISBN 978-1-7252-9796-8 (hardcover) | ISBN 978-1-7252-9797-5 (ebook)

Subjects: LCSH: Christian Life. | Repentance. | Conversion—Christianity.

Classification: BV4501 B76 2021 (paperback) | BV4501 (ebook)

06/18/21

Contents

List of Biblical Books Quoted

Gen	Genesis	Gal	Galatians
Exod	Exodus	Eph	Ephesians
Ps	Psalms	Phil	Philippians
Jer	Jeremiah	Col	Colossians
Ezek	Ezekiel	1 Thess	1 Thessalonians
		2 Tim	2 Timothy
Matt	Matthew	Titus	Titus
Mark	Mark	Heb	Hebrews
Luke	Luke	Jas	James
John	John	1 Pet	1 Peter
Acts	Acts of the Apostles	2 Pet	2 Peter
Rom	Romans	1 John	1 John
1 Cor	1 Corinthians	Rev	Revelation
2 Cor	2 Corinthians		

All biblical translations are by the author.

Introduction

For centuries now, an uninterrupted flow of books, articles, and sermons has attempted to explain the characteristics of the life led by the disciples of Jesus Christ. Some authors begin by examining the figure of Jesus that we find in the four Gospels, for very early on Christians understood their own existence as an *imitatio Christi*. Others attempt to take a more systematic tack, basing their investigation on a particular passage such as the Beatitudes (Matt 5:1–11), the entire Sermon on the Mount (Matt 5–7), or the "fruits of the Spirit" listed by Saint Paul (see Gal 5:22). But almost all of these essays, which often contain excellent intuitions for those who wish to lead a life according to the gospel, concentrate mainly on the *substance* of Christian living. They attempt to provide an answer to the question: "What are the values or character traits that determine an existence in the steps of Christ?"

This line of research, while valuable in itself, often omits another reflection which is equally essential. This other line of questioning focuses, not on the *content* of the life of faith, but on its *form* or shape. Expressed differently, it does not deal with the vocabulary of that life but with its grammar. And just as when we attempt to learn a language, these two dimensions reinforce each other. In order to speak or write a language, we have to know both the meaning of the words and the rules that enable us to assemble them correctly. If we neglect the grammar, even using the right words can lead to misunderstandings.

In these pages, then, I wish to concentrate on what can be called the grammar of the Christian life, essential if the life of believers is to be conformed to that of their Master and mirror a faithful image of it. Otherwise, even the most impressive Christian virtues run the risk of being integrated into a whole that does not awaken us to the breathtaking Newness of God, but merely adds an attractive icing to the cake of a life already well-structured in human terms.

The thesis of this book is that the shape of a life of faith, its basic grammar, can be summed up in a Greek word that we find at the beginning of the Gospel of Jesus Christ—the term *metanoia*, or more exactly the verb *metanoeō*. This notion, however, has to be shorn of many of the extraneous meanings that have adhered to it in the course of centuries and veiled its authentic import. We are perhaps in a position today, more than ever before, of accomplishing this enterprise successfully.

If I may be allowed a personal note here, in writing this work I was all at once struck by the fact that I am carrying forward a topic that has fascinated me from early on. My first publications, written some thirty years ago, were an investigation into the life of faith as a pilgrimage, as a journey in the steps of the pilgrim God. In Jesus, this road enters fully into human history, since it becomes one with a human existence. Other books that followed, on newness or holiness, described the tone or color of this life more than its content. And recently, a long reflection on Holy Saturday as the day that sums up the Christian life in this world attempted to indicate the basic structure of an existence poised between death and life. In the following pages, then, by taking up this leitmotiv once again, I hope to carry it further and deepen our understanding of the specificity and the uniqueness of being a believer at the heart of a world more and more in search of its identity, in which the old answers increasingly fail to convince.

CHAPTER 1

Change Your Outlook!

L et us begin, appropriately, at the beginning. What is this reality we call the Christian faith, which has been around for some two thousand years and taken on a host of forms in the course of its age-old history? A world religion, a way of life, an inner conviction, an institution intimately bound up with the story of Western civilization? All of these things, and many others as well. To focus our vision, let us start by looking at the foundational documents of this faith. The series of writings that Christians call the New Testament begins with four books, generally known as Gospels, which tell the story of the man usually considered as the founder of Christianity: Jesus of Nazareth, a first-century Jew who lived in Palestine and who, after a short career as an itinerant preacher, was arrested and crucified by the Roman occupants for sedition.

Let us focus our vision even more and look at the shortest, and presumably the oldest, of the Gospels, the one entitled *kata Markon*, "according to Mark." Right at the start, after a short introductory section, we find the first words spoken by this man Jesus. By their location and their content, they represent an admirable recapitulation of his message. Although most Bible scholars would not consider them *ipsissima verba* of Jesus, in other words the exact words spoken by him at a specific time and place, it is highly probable that the author of this Gospel chose expressions

I

habitually used by Jesus during his preaching and assembled them to sum up as accurately as possible the essentials of his message.

As far as we know Jesus spoke in Aramaic, the language used by the Jews of Palestine at that time, whereas the Gospels have come down to us written in *koine* Greek, a simplified form of the Hellenic language that served as a common idiom in the eastern Mediterranean world. We are thus already at one remove from the preaching of Jesus himself, and forced to rely on the Gospel writer's understanding of his words. In order not to complicate things and add an additional level of interpretation by simply giving one of the official English versions, we will begin by setting out the Greek text with, underneath, a literal translation of each word. Mark 1:15 tells us that Jesus came to Galilee "proclaiming the good news of God":

				hē basileia tou
peplērōtai	*ho kairos*	*kai*	*ēggiken*	*theou*
	the			
is-filled-up	right-moment	and	has-approached	the reign of God
metanoeite	*kai*	*pisteuete*	*en tōi euangeliōi*	
change-your-				
minds	and	put-your-faith	in the good-news	

The structure of this saying is quite regular in Greek: in the first line, we find two verbs in the perfect indicative tense followed by their subjects and linked by the copula *kai* (and); in the second line, there are two verbs in the present imperative tense, also linked by *kai*. The first part thus announces something that has happened, and indeed is still happening, since the Greek perfect tense expresses a current state of affairs resulting from a past action; the second part invites the hearers to do something in consequence, not just on a single occasion but in an ongoing way (that is the force of the present imperative in Greek).

What in fact has happened? The first clause describes it in very general terms: in simple English, "the time has come." The word *kairos* describes, not a time that flows, but a moment with a particular significance. The verb *plēroō*, "to fill, complete, fulfill," refers to an expectation that has now been satisfied. Previously, this *kairos* was somewhere on the horizon, promised for an indefinite future; it is now close at hand. The seed has ripened and is on the verge of blossoming; the bow is drawn and the arrow is about to take flight.

The second clause makes more explicit what was first expressed in generic terms. This *kairos* is essentially the coming of God's reign or kingdom. Here we find ourselves in a specifically biblical and Jewish context. For the people of Israel at the time of Jesus, the Ruler of all things was the God of the Bible, Creator of the universe, and Father of his people, "a compassionate and generous God, slow to anger and abounding in steadfast love and faithfulness" (Exod 34:6). The problem was that human beings, including those who acknowledged God in theory, did not always accept this rule and live according to the divine precepts. And so the world, instead of being a kingdom of justice and peace, was more often than not a place of confusion and disorder, the locus of all sorts of evils. In consequence, those faithful to God longed for the day when all people would recognize God as their King and live according to God's wishes. If this longing was shared by virtually all of the faithful, there was little agreement as to how God's expected reign would see the light. Would it come suddenly or gradually? Violently or peacefully? Directly from heaven or by means of someone sent for that purpose? Who would be invited to participate? A significant diversity of opinions existed among those who meditated on the history of Israel codified in its sacred books.

And now an itinerant preacher in Galilee, with no apparent credentials, announces that "the Reign of God is at hand." The perfect tense of the verb *engizō*, "to approach, come close," speaks of a reality having come close and which is now in a state of constant closeness. To translate it simply as "has arrived" would miss the nuance expressed by the Greek tense. The expressions "at hand" or "at the door" get closer to this somewhat paradoxical notion of a reality in a permanent state of breaking in. Similarly, we should understand the "time" that "has come" not as a moment, now here, that has inconspicuously taken its place in the series of moments that make up our understanding of time, but as a *kairos* in a permanent state of accessibility. The phrase of the German theologian Paul Tillich, "the eternal now," might help us get a handle on this surprising reality, which pushes our this-worldly categories to the breaking point.

So, according to our preacher, something earth-shattering and totally unprecedented is now in the process of coming about. But rather than give proofs of this startling affirmation or describe it more clearly, Jesus passes from the indicative to the imperative mood: given this new state of affairs, what is to be done? And here too the answer is given by two verbs: *metanoeite kai pisteuete*, "change your outlook and believe" in the message you have heard.

What relationship is there between the two verbs? Is one of them more important than the other? The most obvious solution is to apply to these words the same logic operative in the first sentence. There, we passed from a generic to a more specific description of what is happening. In the same way, we should most probably understand the first verb, *metanoeite*, as the global response required to what God is doing. In classical Greek, the verb *metanoeō* means literally, "to change one's mind." Etymologically, it comes from *nous*, "the mind," and the prefix *meta-*, "after, beyond." It should be pointed out that the word *nous* in Greek denotes a reality somewhat richer than our word "mind." It refers, in short, to the inner life, specifically to what we might call a mindset, the "construal of reality that forms the basis for the prudence (*phronesis*) that guides specific decisions."[1] So the first thing we can affirm is that, in the wake of this new situation which he proclaims, Jesus invites his hearers to a change of heart or to a reorientation of their lives.

Following the logic of the first line, the second part of this phrase specifies more exactly in what this change consists. *Pisteuō* means to believe, that is, to put one's faith or trust (*pistis*) in something or somebody. Here, specifically, it means first of all faith in the good news that Jesus has just proclaimed. Jesus thus explains to his hearers that what is demanded of them is to take utterly

---

1. Johnson, *Among the Gentiles*, 160.

seriously the news they have just heard, in other words to draw from it all the imaginable consequences for the manner in which they think and act. This relationship to the message communicated obviously implies faith, in other words, trust in the messenger, since no other reason is given for undertaking this new way of life.

To sum up, if we see Mark 1:15 as a recapitulation of the basic message of Jesus, then we have a preliminary answer to our question of what it means to be a Christian. God is doing a brand-new thing, and our task is to accept it with the utmost seriousness. And this involves of necessity a radical change in our way of thinking, acting, and being. The New Testament word for this is *metanoia*, which can thus be seen as the essential grammar of the Christian life.

CHAPTER 2

Repentance

The Slide into Moralism

The Gospel thus begins with a call to a radical reorientation of priorities. If we look at the common translations of Mark 1:15 into English, however, we can be forgiven if we fail to grasp the extreme importance of this point. Surprisingly, all the major English versions of the Bible render *metanoeite* as "repent."[1] The Shorter Oxford English Dictionary's definition of this word is to "feel contrition or regret for something one has done or omitted to do; change one's mind through regret about past action or conduct; view or think of an action with dissatisfaction and regret." How did such an inexact and tendentious translation come to be accepted?

The shift began a long time ago, when the New Testament was translated from Greek into Latin. The Latin Vulgate was the official Bible for centuries in the West. And in the text from Mark's Gospel we are examining, the verb *metanoeō* was translated by *paeniteo* or

1. The only exceptions I have come across are the *Complete Jewish Bible* ("turn to God from your sins"); *New International Reader's Version* ("turn away from your sins"); *Young's Literal Translation* ("reform ye"); *God's Word Translation* ("change the way you think and act"). The first three, it should be noted, still maintain the negative focus expressed by the word "repent." Similarly, in the Eastern Church the word *metanoia* refers to bowing and touching the floor as a sign of repentance.

poeniteo, "to cause to regret, make sorry." Aside from "repent," the Latin root gives us words like "penitent," "penance," "penitentiary," all with a negative and highly moral connotation.

To be fair, it should be admitted that this nuance is not absent from the Greek and so the translation is not totally unfounded. To change one's mind can often involve regret for one's previous convictions, and in classical Greek the word is occasionally used with this shade of meaning. Likewise, in the Greek translation of the Hebrew Scriptures, the so-called Septuagint, *metanoeō* is sometimes used to translate *nḥm*, which among its various meanings we find "to regret, repent." However, there is another Greek verb which fits this semantic slot more exactly, namely *metamelomai* (see Matt 21:32). And most often in the Septuagint, *metanoeō* is used for another Hebrew verb, *shuv*, meaning "to turn around," a term often used by the prophets of Israel to call the nation to return to God.

This notion of a "turning" obviously corresponds well with the primary meaning of *metanoeō*, namely a change in perception and decision. In both cases, the accent is placed on the *movement* from one state of affairs to another. One turns *away* from something in order to turn *towards* something else. In specific cases, either the starting point or the end point may be emphasized, but the most important thing is the dynamic quality, the movement, the passing from A to B. If we examine the uses of *metanoeō* and *metanoia* in the New Testament, we see that sometimes A is mentioned (turning from) and sometimes B (turning towards), but the accent is clearly on the change. So, for instance, people are encouraged to turn away from their wickedness (Acts 8:22), from their dead works (Heb 6:1), from the works of their hands and their sins (Rev 9:20–21; cf. 2:21–22; 16:11; Luke 5:32). But more often than not, it is the positive goal that is invoked. In the footsteps of John the Baptist (Mark 1:4; Luke 3:3), Jesus offers a *metanoia* that leads to liberation from sin (Luke 24:47; Acts 2:38; 3:19; cf. 5:31), to life (Acts 11:18), salvation (2 Cor 7:10), and knowledge of the truth (2 Tim 2:25). And most generally in the New Testament, *metanoia* is simply affirmed as a reality desirable in itself, a radical change of heart, and therefore of behavior. This transformation was signified by John's baptism (Matt 3:11; Acts 13:24; 19:4), brought about by God's kindness (Rom 2:4) and patience (2 Pet 3:9), and proclaimed by the disciples of Jesus (Mark 6:12). Commanded by God (Acts 17:30), *metanoia* is an inner explosion of energy (Rev 3:19, "zeal") that involves "faith in our Lord Jesus" (Acts 20:21) and a turning towards God (Acts 26:20). Without this inward change, there is nothing to hope for (Matt 11:20–24; 12:41; Luke 13:3,5).

The biblical background enables us to see just what is wrong with the translation of *metanoia* as "repentance." The English word drastically shifts the center of gravity from the movement forward to a fixation on what was left behind. It places the accent on remorse for one's past errors and the experience of repugnance, replacing a dynamic advance with a static and negative emotion. It is true that regret can sometimes motivate a change of life, but taken in itself it can just as often lead to depression and despair, if one does not find the energy to change course and set out anew.

The true course of *metanoia* stands out clearly in two well-known parables of Jesus:

> The Kingdom of heaven is like treasure hidden in a field, which someone found and hid. In his joy he went off and sold all he had and bought that field. Again, the Kingdom of heaven is like a merchant in search of beautiful pearls. When he found one of great value, he went off and sold all he had and bought it. (Matt 13:44–46)

It is the discovery of the treasure or the pearl that motivates the entire process, providing the impulse for a radical transformation of one's life.

Remorse for the past finds its authentic place not before, but *after* the experience of *metanoia*. When a person has made the leap and discovered a new life through an encounter with Christ, he or she can then look back and measure the distance covered and the time lost, echoing the well-known words of Saint Augustine: "Too late have I loved you, O Beauty ancient and always new!"[2] But this

---

2. *Conf.* 10.27.

is more properly a result of the life-giving encounter with God, and not a prelude to it.

The insufficiency, not to say the error, of the translation of *metanoia* as repentance has often been noted. Already in the second century, the Christian thinker Tertullian (155–240), who incidentally had written an entire treatise on repentance, admitted: "Now in Greek the word for repentance is derived, not from the confession of sin, but from a change of mind."[3]

Closer to us, in the late nineteenth century, an Episcopal priest in Boston, Treadwell Walden (1830–1918), wrote an essay on the subject, which he later expanded into a book. Asking himself, "How did such an extraordinary mistranslation get into our New Testament?"[4] Walden set out at great length all the arguments against it. He then sent his essay to those in charge of revising the official English New Testament at that time, hoping that it would effect a change. Surprisingly, although everyone seemed to agree with his conclusions, such a modification was thought impossible, since the committee felt that the word "repentance" had become part of the Christian vocabulary to such an extent that it had to be retained, leaving it up to preachers and teachers to explain its true meaning for the Gospel. In addition, no suitable alternative seemed readily at hand.

Unfortunately, such arguments have simply prolonged the basic misunderstanding. For as Walden himself pointed out, it is not merely a matter of giving a more precise meaning to a multivalent or ambiguous term; the word itself points in the wrong direction. It expresses and confirms a shift that began very early in the Christian era and has rendered problematic for many the discovery of the authentic import of the Gospel—the slide into moralism.

How is it that a doctrine, the essence of which is to proclaim God's indefectible love for humanity despite all the missteps and refusals that have marked the human condition from the beginning,

3. *Nam et in Graeco sono paenitentiae nomen non ex delicti confessione, sed ex animi demutatione compositum est.* Tertullian, *Marc.* 2.24.

4. Walden, *Metanoia*, 24.

has been so often transformed in the course of Christian centuries into its polar opposite: an irrevocable condemnation of human beings, an emphasis on their utter unworthiness and an exhortation to them to do the impossible in order to deserve this love? How did it come about that grace, the utterly undeserved and free gift bestowed by Jesus, the spokesperson for God, was transmuted into a law without appeal, to which no one can apparently ever measure up?

The question is a complex one, because no one can deny that faith has an ethical or moral dimension: one cannot call oneself a Christian if one accepts certain ideas but is not disposed to act in consequence, forsaking a self-centered outlook to attempt to live with and for God and others. What is here referred to as moralism, however, is not simply the call to a good life but rather a fixation on human sinfulness, an exaggerated focus on wrongdoing, guilt and the condemnation of misbehavior and error. Such an outlook reduces the gospel to a set of rules to regulate action, and every shortcoming, however trivial, is seen as invalidating a person's claim to enjoy fellowship with the divine. This pessimistic attitude can easily engender scrupulosity and undermine the joy which is the hallmark of the Christian life.

Where did this turn to moralism come from? When did it begin? The French Protestant thinker and social critic Jacques Ellul (1912–94) has a chapter in his book, *The Subversion of Christianity*, entitled "Moralism," in which he analyzes this phenomenon in detail. He concludes that it is the result of two developments: first, the passage of Christianity from the faith of a small minority living an intense community life "in the Spirit" to a religion of the masses and, simultaneously, periods of widespread immorality in Western society, notably from the fourth to the seventh centuries and in the fourteenth and fifteenth centuries. Confronted with these situations, Christian leaders were almost inevitably led to emphasize norms and rules to be followed.[5] "The perversion, then, was that

5. A telling example of this is the transformation of Mary of Magdala from the friend of Jesus and the "apostle to the apostles" to the repentant prostitute in the homilies of Pope Gregory the Great (540–604). See Landrivon,

of making the gospel into law in order to respond to the challenge offered to revelation by the successive outbursts of immorality and ethical disorder."[6] Another French thinker, the historian Jean Delumeau, emphasizes a related turn of events: the growth of fear and anguish in the late Middle Ages, with its effects on the religious sensibility of Europeans. "No civilization has ever attached as much importance to guilt and shame as did the Western world from the thirteenth to the eighteenth centuries."[7] Events such as the Great Plague of the fourteenth century, which exterminated up to half of Europe's population, and the Thirty Years' War in the seventeenth century undoubtedly helped to create an cultural climate of widespread pessimism and hopelessness. This may well have brought to the fore those aspects of the Christian faith that emphasized human sinfulness and "contempt of the world," seen as a vale of tears.

These sociological and historical considerations, however, only point to a deeper and more specifically theological misunderstanding: an insufficient grasp of the message of the founder of Christianity, beginning with the understanding of the identity of the *Abba* of Jesus the Christ. The "god" believed in and worshipped by holders of this moralistic outlook remains the supreme Judge, more concerned with condemning sin and punishing the guilty than offering, out of pure love, undeserved and unimaginable happiness to all. This god demands unending attempts to purge oneself of evil rather than openness to the good news of unconditional forgiveness and the willingness to live one's life in consequence. Ironically, the understanding of *metanoia* as repentance is a clear sign of the absence of true *metanoia*—we continue to place sin at the center of our consciousness and not the love that makes possible constant new beginnings. Without God's help, a clear-sighted vision of our world certainly offers a host of reasons to despair, but that is not the question. The slide into moralism is

"L'Écriture mythologisée."

6. Ellul, *Subversion of Christianity*, 89.

7. Delumeau, *Sin and Fear*, 3. See also his earlier and related work *La Peur en Occident*.

essentially a backsliding into a pre-Christian mentality in homage to the vindictive gods of this world, and a largely unconscious refusal to enter into the new world opened up by the resurrection of the Messiah.

CHAPTER 3

Conversion

The Slide into Triumphalism

The other common translation of *metanoeō/metanoia*, favored by most of the Bibles in the Romance languages, is "to convert/conversion." This translation sets us at once on firmer ground.[1] The Latin verb *vertere* means "to turn," and so conversion is literally a turning round, a movement from and to. Although not exactly equivalent to the Greek term, it does render very closely the Hebrew verb *shuv*, which as we have seen has the primary meaning of "to turn about, to return" and is used in the Hebrew Scriptures to describe a turning from false gods and inauthentic behavior to the God of Israel and the stipulations of the covenant with that deity.

The literal Greek translation of *shuv* would be *epistrephō* and, significantly, that verb is sometimes used as a synonym for *metanoeō* in the New Testament, notably in the Acts of the Apostles (Acts 9:35; 11:21: 14:15; 15:19; 26:18; cf. 1 Thess 1:9). Twice, *epistrephō* is even set into parallel with *metanoeō*: "Change your hearts and turn so that your sins may be wiped out. . . . I enjoined the Gentiles to change their hearts and turn to God, doing deeds

---

1. A similar evolution is found in the German Bibles, where the older expression *Buße tun* (to repent, do penance) has been replaced in the modern translations by *umkehren* (to turn around).

worthy of this change" (Acts 3:19; 26:20). *Metanoia* can thus correctly be seen as a conversion, if this is understood in the literal sense of a turning away from one's old way of thinking and acting and a turning towards a new outlook and behavior.

It must be said, however, that the term "conversion" has likewise become problematic for a correct understanding of *metanoia*, not because of the word itself, but because of the connotations that have clung to it over the centuries. The Shorter Oxford English Dictionary, after giving as a first definition of conversion "the turning of sinners to God," continues with "the action of bringing a person over, or the fact of being brought over, to a particular belief or opinion, specifically to a religious faith." Religious conversion has come to mean becoming an adherent of a particular religion, often with the implicit notion that one has left one's old network of relationships to join a new social group, usually a Christian church or sect. It is not for nothing that such a person is known as a "convert." From an inner transformation, conversion has changed its meaning to refer to a shift of religious allegiance, generally considered a once-and-for-all occurrence. Still worse for a true understanding of *metanoia*, the verb "to convert" has acquired the additional meaning of "doing what is necessary to bring about this change of allegiance in others." So it became possible to speak of missionaries being sent out to "convert" the heathens or the Jews, whether for altruistic or self-interested motives, and whether employing honorable or deceitful tactics. Here it is obvious that we are very far from the New Testament notion of *metanoia*, which can only refer to a change which takes place in the depths of a person's being, in a climate of inner freedom. "What fascinates in God is his humility. God never punishes, never domineers nor wounds human dignity. Any authoritarian gesture on our part disfigures his face and repels. As for Christ, 'poor and humble of heart'—he never forces anyone's hand. If he forced himself upon you, I would not be inviting you to follow him."[2]

The sociological dimension of *metanoia*, although present from the beginning, has led to another grave misunderstanding

2. Roger of Taizé, *Wonder of a Love*, 104.

regarding the meaning of faith in Jesus as the Messiah. When the first Christians came to faith, this was made concrete in a change in their outward status, a shift in their reference group. They left behind their past associations and joined a community of like-minded believers with a lifestyle radically different from that of the people around them and of society at large. As Saint Paul put it in his Letter to the Colossians:

> [God] has saved us from the power of darkness and transferred us into the Kingdom of his beloved Son, in whom we have redemption, the forgiveness of sins. (Col 1:13–14)

To the extent, however, that this change of social status became identified with the act of "conversion," it led to the understanding of *metanoia* as a once-and-for-all occurrence that separates a person from the rest of humankind and places him or her definitively among the "saved." "The Kingdom of his beloved Son" is identified with the Christian community, the church as a historical institution, and a person within its embrace is considered as different in quality from his or her fellow human beings. The New Testament images of a "new birth" (cf. John 1:13; 3:3–8; Rom 8:29; Col 1:18; 1 Pet 1:3,23; Jas 1:18; Rev 1:5) and a "new self" (Eph 4:24; Col 3:10) reinforced this understanding of salvation. And so, when the Christian church, in a relatively short time, historically speaking, radically changed its shape and went from being a tiny network of house communities to becoming the official religion of the Roman Empire, backed by the power of the State, Christianity was well on its way to being seen as the one true religion, alongside which others were persecuted at worst and tolerated at best.

Thus was born what may be called the heresy of triumphalism. I am using the term here to refer to a vision of the faith whereby Christians see themselves as people who have already found salvation; they have already crossed over to the other side. Merely by being members of the church, they possess the Truth. They are thus separated from the rest of their fellows, still wallowing in the mud of error, by a chasm which can only be crossed if the others come to their senses and follow their lead. Ironically, such a representation of believers is closer to the portrayal of the Pharisees, "the separated ones," in the gospels, generally seen by Christians as being the adversaries of Jesus. From what we know of the Pharisees today, however, we realize that they were closer to the outlook of Jesus than was often thought. In order to hasten the coming of God's Reign, they felt that it was imperative to begin here and now by living as if God were already sovereign, by following the precepts of the Law to the fullest possible extent. They had consequently to "take the yoke of the Torah upon their shoulders," as they expressed it. This laudable endeavor brought with it, however, the unfortunate tendency to see themselves as the righteous and the pure, and to distance themselves from "the people of the land" in order not to be contaminated.

In the same way, Christians have often seen the gift of faith they have received as placing them in a privileged position. Even if they do not boast about their superiority, but wish to extend it to their still-benighted contemporaries, they still unconsciously view themselves as being fundamentally different from others. Without realizing it, they apply to themselves the words of Saint Paul concerning his fellow Jews:

> [You] consider yourself to be a guide of the blind, a light
> for those in darkness, an instructor of the ignorant,
> a teacher of the immature, possessing the epitome of
> knowledge and truth in the Law. (Rom 2:19–20)

Viewing the Torah as a possession rather than the gift of a source of life for all, they attempt to teach others without realizing that they themselves have just as much to learn and to receive.

In the past, when Christianity still benefited from an alliance with the State, this attitude could lead to attempts to coerce others into accepting the faith "for their own good." Today, fortunately, the Inquisition is behind us, but a triumphalistic outlook is still present in a host of subtler ways. It reveals itself in those bitter fights over orthodoxy, where those who are not sufficiently rooted in the tradition of the church or not correctly "born again" are consigned to the outer darkness. It likewise becomes visible in the refusal to take seriously the seeds of hope present in contemporary culture and in other human traditions and, more importantly, the unwillingness to learn from the achievements of others outside the fold. It is present, in short, wherever faith leads to feelings of superiority and a destruction of the bonds of solidarity with others.

Like all heresies, triumphalism is based on a genuine truth which has been wrested out of its context and made absolute. Faith is indeed a gift from God, and it cannot by its nature remain exterior to the person who welcomes it; it transforms us from within, starting from the depths of our being. Through God's Spirit we are reborn to a new life in Christ, and become part of a new community. And it is equally true, as we shall see, that the first stage of *metanoia*, expressed sacramentally in baptism, is a privileged moment that recapitulates the entire Christian life. But just as with the slide into moralism, triumphalism is rooted in an insufficient understanding of who the God of Jesus Christ is. The result of the gift of faith can never be to detach us from others, creating an "in-group" looking down with haughtiness or pity upon the others. On the contrary, faith is a gift of solidarity, in the steps of Jesus "who, though he was of divine condition, did not consider equality with God a privilege to be clung to but emptied himself, taking on the condition of a slave, being born in human likeness" (Phil 2:6–7).

In recent years, the Christian church has passed through trials that have radically called into question its supposed moral superiority. The crisis caused by abuses of power, in the sexual as well as in the financial domains, has sounded the death knell concerning any "clerical" or "authoritarian" view of an institution wishing to impose its vision on others. Will we learn from these events, seeing them as a providential and salutary warning by which God attempts to place us back in the straight and narrow path of the gospel?

Triumphalism errs fundamentally in its view of *metanoia* as a once-and-for-all occurrence, a "conversion" that places us already on the mountaintop. Put another way, it can be defined as a total identification of our empirical being, always on the road, with the gift we have received; in the final analysis, it is thus a refusal of history. The divine presence or Spirit is thus no longer seen as a gift with transforming power; it has become something that belongs to us and that we can manage and control as we wish. Instead of letting ourselves constantly be called out of our routines towards the horizon of God's kingdom, what we call "faith" has apparently been integrated into an existence where our self is still firmly in charge. In short, the living God is well on the way to becoming an idol.

What is the way out of this dead end? Triumphalism is not eliminated by a kind of indifference, by relativizing the importance and the radical nature of life in Christ. Such an undertaking would rob the gospel of its reason for being. Triumphalism can only be overcome by understanding the life of faith not as something attained once and for all, but as a constantly repeated movement from death to life in the company of the risen Jesus. In his Letter to the Philippians, Saint Paul describes how his life is a sharing in the death and resurrection of Christ (Phil 3:10–11). Then he writes, using the image of a race:

> Not that I have already received [the prize] or have already reached perfection, but I keep running forward in order to take hold of it, since I have been taken hold of by Christ Jesus. I do not imagine, my brothers and sisters, that I have taken hold, but what I say is this: forgetting what lies behind me and straining towards what lies ahead, I run towards the goal to get the prize—God's heavenly calling in Christ Jesus. (Phil 3:12–13)

And the apostle continues, with an ironic twist:

> Those of us who are "perfect" should have this attitude; if any of you see things differently, God will reveal this to you too. (Phil 3:15)

In other words, the only way to be a perfect Christian is to know that one is still on the road![3]

3. "Here below to live is to change, and to be perfect is to have changed often." Newman, *Development*, 40 (1.1.1.7).

And this means, as an inevitable corollary, that we remain in solidarity with all the others walking along that road, at whatever point they may be: "In the meantime, let us march forward all together in conformity with what we have attained" (Phil 3:16). In so doing, we are in the image of Jesus, whose first public act was to go down into the waters of the Jordan in the company of all those who were acknowledging their sinfulness and imploring the divine pardon. And filled with the Spirit after this baptism, Jesus was not brought to some quiet mountaintop far from his fellows to enjoy intimacy with God in serene isolation. He was led instead by the Spirit out into the wilderness, to wrestle on our behalf with the forces of darkness. Following Christ can never be a privilege; it is a path of incarnation, bringing us into a deeper fellowship with all our brothers and sisters—and indeed with all that exists. Those who possess the Spirit of the Messiah groan in company with the groaning of all creation in the process of giving birth (cf. Rom 8:22–23).

CHAPTER 4

The Adventure

Our discussion of how the word *metanoia* is habitually translated in our New Testaments has established two things concerning what it is not. First of all, *metanoia* is not a backward-looking activity, centered on an obsessive regret for our mistakes followed by a promise, more often than not fruitless, to do better in the future. Rather than describing a negative and moralistic attitude, it is forward-looking and dynamic, a reorientation of one's entire being to move ahead in the company of Christ. Secondly, although it is lived out differently in each stage of a person's existence, *metanoia* is not a once-and-for-all phenomenon that simply coincides with a change of outward condition, notably that of joining or belonging to a Christian community or church. It is an ongoing process that turns the believer into a person on the move.

Let us now attempt to discern more clearly the positive shape of this activity, process, or attitude that is called *metanoia*. A first question has to do with its beginning. What sets it in motion? What makes it possible?

If we return to the text we examined earlier, at the beginning of Mark's Gospel, we see that the starting point for the change is the announcement of some "good news." Jesus tells his hearers that what the nation has been awaiting for centuries is now about to take place; he further implies that this is not something that will happen independently of them, but requires their active participation. The following passage shows what this means concretely in the lives of four ordinary men:

> Walking beside the Sea of Galilee, he saw Simon and his brother Andrew casting their nets into the sea, for they were fishermen. Jesus said to them, "Come with me, and I will make you fishers of people." At once they left their nets and followed him. A little further on he saw James the son of Zebedee and John his brother in the boat repairing their nets. Immediately he called them. And leaving their father Zebedee in the boat with his hired hands, they came after him. (Mark 1:16–20; Matt 4:18–22)

The proclamation here takes the form of a *call*, a call containing a promise: "Come with me, and I will make you fishers of people." At this point in the story it is not very clear to the reader, no more than it was to the first disciples, what this promise entails; it is enough for now to see it as a widening and deepening of their present occupation. Some ordinary "fishers" are invited to become "fishers of people." A new future opens up before them, obviously linked to the proclamation of the Reign of God.

This passage shows us quite dramatically that the men who are thus called immediately leave everything behind—family, work, and home—to set out with Jesus. There was thus something in them that responded to the invitation, implicitly viewing it as more important than all the other choices and relationships they had previously known. Put another way, this word that came to them from without, from the lips of Jesus, revealed a deeper place within them, unsuspected until then—what Saint Augustine calls the *interior intimo meo*, a place more inward than our innermost being[1]—that henceforth became the motivating force of their personality.

In the other Gospels, the call is not quite so direct. In chapter 5 of Luke's Gospel, Jesus asks Simon first of all to lend him his boat so he can preach without being crushed by the crowd. Shortly

---

1. Augustine, *Conf.* 3.6, 11.

afterwards, a new stage begins with the disconcerting command, "Head out into deep water and let down your nets for a catch" (Luke 5:4). The preacher apparently takes it into his head to give fishing lessons to fishermen! Whereas previously only a minimum of good will was required to do a favor for an illustrious man, now something more is needed—an act of pure trust in the face of the unknown. The miraculous catch of fish that ensues awakens in Simon a profound reaction of unworthiness, characteristic of an encounter with the divine, and leads to the call and the response. The contrast between the shallow water at the beginning of the story and the deep water which follows is a dramatic illustration of the difference between Simon's everyday life before the encounter with Jesus and the unsuspected depths which this encounter opens up within him.

In John's Gospel, the first disciples are attracted to Jesus by the testimony of John the Baptizer (John 1:35–37). They listen to Jesus and spend time with him. In their turn, they then go and tell others what they have seen and heard (1:40–42). The encounter with Jesus mediated through another person is especially characteristic of the post-paschal situation of believers. Jesus is no longer present as a human being who calls us with his human voice. We meet him now in other persons and events which serve as a catalyst for an encounter. And since the Christian community, the church, has the mission of continuing Christ's work in the world, the most normal way to receive a call is through the witness of Christians, either individually or collectively, by means of actions or of words, whether spoken or written. The day may come when one of these things touches a given person's heart and reveals to them a previously unknown dimension of life, a deeper meaning, which unsettles them and calls for a new response. Since the ways of God are manifold, it is not even necessary that the first call come from an explicitly Christian source. The first revelatory impulse may be an experience of beauty, of wonder at nature, an intense human relationship, or a host of other things. At some point, however, the person has to grasp the connection between his or her personal experience and the story told in the New Testament and continued in the life of Christians, so that the call can be recognized as a call and a conscious and voluntary response offered.[2] What is essential is that a message coming from outside an individual, amidst the commonplace conditions of earthly existence, awaken an inner desire that seems more authentic than anything that individual has previously known.

We find this same suggestive link between an outward event and a radical response from within in an essay written in 1911, which has no explicit connection to Christianity. It is all the more astonishing that this article provides an excellent phenomenological description of the grammar of faith. Its author was Georg Simmel (1858–1918), one of the first generation of German sociologists, and the essay in question was entitled *"Das Abenteuer"* ("The Adventure").[3]

Simmel attempts to give a phenomenological description of a particular type of event he calls "an adventure" and of the kind of person who undertakes it ("the adventurer"). The experience in question is characterized by a unique link between an outward and an inward reality. Simmel does not use the word "call" to describe the outer reality, since he is not limiting himself to a specifically religious context. He speaks rather of an event outside the "continuity of life." Such an event leads to an adventure, when the protagonist discovers in this "accident" an inner necessity that comes from "the unifying core of existence from which meaning flows." The adventure is "a foreign body in our existence which is yet somehow connected with the center." This creates a particular way of living, one detached from the ordinary flow of time, with a

2. This is where problems often arise today, especially among intellectually oriented persons. In an age where a multitude of worldviews coexist more or less peacefully, the idea of privileging one particular narrative and seeing it as normative for one's own inner journey cannot but appear outlandish to many. This is sometimes articulated as the difference between "religion," a sociological reality, and "spirituality," a personal quest. It should be emphasized that such a separation between the social and the personal dimensions of existence, while characteristic of contemporary society, is fundamentally alien to the message of Jesus.

3. Simmel, "Abenteuer." I have taken the following quotations from the unpaged online English translation.

specific beginning and end; it is a life rooted in the present, independent of the "before" and "after" of normal existence.

The adventure as described by Simmel unites activity and passivity, certainty and uncertainty, the purposeful and the arbitrary. A particular example he chooses to illustrate this is that of a love-affair, primarily from the masculine side. There is both a sense of "fate" or "grace" in having discovered the beloved, and an impulse to act in order to win and keep her. The artist and the gambler are other examples of this endeavor. The adventurer must make use of all his faculties, while at the same time abandoning himself to life-forces beyond his control. In a particularly compelling phrase, Simmel defines the adventurer as someone who "makes a system of life out of his life's lack of system."

A typical adventure may be quite fleeting in time and yet be seen to have timeless validity. But our author also states that "life as a whole may be perceived as an adventure." For this to occur, however, "one must sense above its totality a higher unity, a super-life, as it were." We have here an essentially religious attitude, since Simmel goes on to say:

> Certain religious moods seem to bring about such a perception. When our earthly career strikes us as a mere preliminary phase in the fulfillment of eternal destinies, when we have no home but merely a temporary asylum on earth, this obviously is only a particular variant of the general feeling that life as a whole is an adventure.

This is as far as this highly suggestive essay goes. But hopefully one can see how this analysis provides a possible underpinning in human psychology and sociology for a life according to the gospel. In the seemingly accidental and arbitrary event of the birth of a man in Palestine two thousand years ago, and in a host of other events that followed from this, an inner call or desire was awakened in countless individuals. It provided them with a meaning that took them out of the banality and the routines of the ordinary and gave their existence a brand-new significance, one needing to be discovered day by day. From that moment on, they entered upon the adventure of faith.

A complementary approach to gain an understanding of the logic of *metanoia* comes from biography. In the lives of some renowned men and women, one can see with exceptional clarity the way certain events, even apparently insignificant or unfavorable ones, lead to profound changes in their understanding and action, again and again. This is not to say that *metanoia* is the exclusive attribute of a spiritual elite. By its very nature it is offered to all. But many of us are like sleepwalkers much of the time, caught up in the routines that make existence possible and even agreeable; we submit to life like pebbles tossed by the surf. For most people, a fully conscious and voluntary response to what is perceived as a call is a relatively rare occurrence, generally limited to a particularly dramatic moment in their lives. Once that moment has passed, they often lapse back into their usual behavior, ruled by habit and custom. Some individuals, on the other hand, derive from such experiences a basic attitude that continues to mark their way of life. They become adventurers of the spirit, and so their existence has sign-value for the rest of us.

A particularly telling example, even more suggestive because it took place outside of the Christian framework, is the life of the man known as Malcolm X (1925–65).[4] Born Malcolm Little in an African American family in the Midwest of the United States, as a young man he moved to the East Coast, where he quickly became a delinquent and a minor criminal until he ended up in prison in 1946. There, he experienced the first of his "conversions." A fellow prisoner taught him to read and think for himself, and he became interested in a group called the Nation of Islam, popularly known as the Black Muslims, which preached an extremely idiosyncratic form of Islam advocating black self-reliance and a blanket rejection of white America and the policy of integration. Upon leaving prison in 1952, Malcolm went to meet Elijah Muhammed, the

4. In what follows see especially *The Autobiography of Malcolm X*. First published in 1965, it has become a classic. For a fuller and more objective account, see Marable, *Malcolm X*. This more critical although still fair-handed treatment plays the role of the modern quest for the historical Jesus as compared to the New Testament gospels, although this obviously in no way implies any equivalence between Malcolm X and Jesus of Nazareth.

head of the sect, and soon became a leading figure in the Nation of Islam, reputed for the strength and quality of his convictions, his speaking ability, and his impeccable lifestyle.

At the same time as he was working tirelessly for the Nation of Islam, Malcolm began increasingly to have doubts about the sect, due both to its policies and beliefs as well as to the character of its leader. This led to another major "conversion," by which he broke with the Black Muslims and the man he considered a second father to him. He then entered a period of searching, during which he became an orthodox Sunni Muslim and made a pilgrimage to Mecca, another life-changing experience. He returned from Mecca with a new name, el-Hajj Malik el-Shabazz, and a new outlook, having seen that people of all colors, races, and backgrounds could live together based on their faith in Allah. He founded a mosque in New York and an organization for Afro-American unity, and traveled and lectured widely. While he was in this transitional period, a time when his new convictions were still gradually taking shape, he was assassinated in Harlem, New York, ostensibly by members of the Black Muslims, although doubts still remain concerning the exact circumstances of his death.

Obviously, similar examples could have been found within the Christian world, beginning with Saul of Tarsus, the man who became Saint Paul for Christians. Yet choosing someone from another frame of reference, particularly someone whose ideas would not be shared by most Christian believers, allows us to see more clearly the *structure* of a life independently of its specific *content*, to grasp its grammar rather than its vocabulary. Malcolm X was second to none in his ability to evolve and grow inwardly as a result of personal encounters and experiences. In addition to what we have identified as his major changes of direction, there were a host of smaller events taken as indications of a road to follow. His life, truly an adventure as described by Georg Simmel, helps us to see that "conversion" is not a once-and-for-all phenomenon, but that a life of *metanoia* involves countless moments where outward occurrences, large or small, are seen as calls to a reorientation of the personality, the road towards a greater and deeper life.

CHAPTER 5

Baptized into Christ

What the New Testament refers to as *metanoia* is thus, in its essence, a complex interaction between something external to a person and a movement deep within. Particular events or encounters, more or less contingent and arbitrary in human terms, touch something in the depths of a man or woman that seems to them more real than anything they have yet known. Although they may not necessarily use the term, especially at first, in the event or encounter they come to hear a *call* inviting them to respond by changing the shape of their existence. Discerning the call and responding to it are expressions of a basic act of trust, which the New Testament names faith: the call is considered worthwhile and important enough to motivate a new beginning in one's life, to reconsider in its light all one's previous values and choices.

In more specifically Christian terms, in and through the often mundane happenings of their life believers discern a call from Christ, through whom God speaks to them. Although the event or encounter is in itself contingent, the call witnesses to an Absolute that is not. It comes from God, the Source of all, and thus is able to awaken or reveal something within a person that likewise partakes of the Absolute, a dimension or place that is not subject to the fluctuations and hesitations of ordinary human life. "Deep calls to deep" (Ps 42:7). This inner space is the locus of a deep desire, and from it surges a response, a YES, that is unconditional. How this unconditional YES is lived out in the changeable and unpredictable circumstances of human life defines the particular challenge of believing and gives it its sometimes dramatic flavor.

In John's Gospel, Jesus uses a parable to elucidate the process that has just been described, the discernment of a call from Christ that evokes a spontaneous response arising from the depths of our being. As he often does in his preaching, Jesus takes a common example of his day, that of a shepherd and his sheep:

> The one who enters through the gate is the shepherd of the sheep. The gatekeeper opens the gate for him; the sheep hear his voice and he calls his own sheep by name and leads them out. When he has brought all his own sheep out, he walks ahead and the sheep follow him, because they recognize his voice. They would not follow a stranger but instead they would run away from him, because they do not recognize the voice of strangers. (John 10:2–5)

This simple image shows how a stimulus from without, when it is heard and then recognized as "the master's voice," has the power to evoke an unreflective response. Because of the trust between the shepherd and "his own sheep," they follow him spontaneously, rather than out of a fear of negative consequences or because the shepherd entices them with good things. They are intimately acquainted with him, and therefore implicitly realize that their true good lies in this relationship. They know him because he knows them: he calls them "by name," as unique persons created by God for a relationship. Only the Shepherd knows our true name, our true identity, and it is his call that reveals it to us. The question posed by this little parable, then, is not "How do we follow Jesus?" but rather "How do we hear and recognize that voice calling us by our name in the midst of all the noise that surrounds and distracts us?"

We should note that, in this image of the shepherd and his sheep, a relationship between them already exists beforehand. And this enables us to go further with a question we examined earlier.

Against the error of triumphalism, of believing we have already arrived and viewing faith as a static reality or a permanent condition,
metanoia was presented as a continuous process and not a once-
and-for-all reality. At this point, however, we need to introduce
some distinctions. Although *metanoia* is the shape of the entire
Christian life and not just its starting-point, it inevitably passes
through successive stages in the course of a believer's lifetime.

A key moment in this process is unquestionably the first
time that a call from God is heard and recognized for what it is,
evoking the response of faith and leading to outward changes in a
person's life. As we saw earlier, this is what is traditionally known
as "conversion." It is good to realize, however, that this first stage
is not necessarily a one-time event occurring out of the blue, coming at a particular time and place. Although some individuals may
experience an impressive encounter with the divine with a power
and an intensity that cause their entire previous existence to pale
by comparison, upon closer inspection it almost always becomes
clear that the encounter was preceded by a series of events that
paved the way for it. Saint Paul may have focused on his earth-
shattering meeting with the risen Jesus on the road to Damascus
(see Acts 9:1–19; 22:3–21; 26:9–18) and considered his previous
attainments "garbage" (Phil 3:8), but with the benefit of hindsight
we can view his past life as a Pharisee, passionately concerned with
the things of God, as a providential preparation for the new calling
he would receive.

Many people, in fact, do see their life previous to receiving
the gift of faith as merely a series of false steps and aimless wan-
dering. Others, however, looking back on their past in the light
of the present, see that they were being led, most often unawares,
towards a goal they could not yet imagine. The literature of conversion abounds with such descriptions of a gradual journey towards
the light, unrecognized by the person at the time and clear only
once the definitive step had been taken.[1] From a theological point

1. Some modern autobiographies of faith, in this sense, are Lewis, *Surprised by Joy* (originally published in 1955); Day, *Long Loneliness* (originally
published in 1952); Merton, *Seven Storey Mountain* (originally published in

of view, this latter outlook is the more accurate one. Spiritual autobiography is an authentic literary genre because the retrospective glance is a fundamental aspect of the journey of faith, shown emblematically in the cry of the disciples on the road to Emmaus, "Were not our hearts on fire within us when he was speaking to us on the road?" (Luke 24:32).[2] Christ was there all the time, but they did not consciously realize it. Is this not the meaning of the famous words the French thinker Blaise Pascal (1623–62) attributed to Jesus: "You would not be looking for me if you had not already found me"?[3] The only absolutely new beginning in the pilgrimage of faith comes from the side of God; as humans we are inevitably already on the road.

This being said, a key stage in the process of *metanoia* is the moment when one first consciously becomes aware of the real presence of the Absolute in one's life, understood as an invitation requiring a response, and when one says yes to it. This event recapitulates, as it were, the basic structure of the Christian life. From the time of the first Christians it was attached to a particular rite, that of baptism. In general, a woman or man was attracted to the Christian life through the example of other believers, and at a certain time saw this way of life as the one thing that mattered, compared to which all else seemed secondary. As a result, they chose to leave their former life behind and join the Christian community, which often involved a radical break with family, friends, and their previous occupation. Following a time of preparation, necessary both to allow the believer to enter more deeply into the meaning of this new life and to verify his or her readiness, Christ's call and the believer's response was expressed sacramentally by an act of immersion ("baptism"): an image of dying and rising to a new life with Christ (Rom 6:3–4), of acquiring a new identity (changing

---

1948). Such works continue a long tradition which arguably began with the *Confessions* of Saint Augustine of Hippo (354–430).

2. This perspective is also that of John's Gospel: "His disciples did not understand these things at first, but when Jesus was glorified they remembered that these things had been written about him" (John 12:16; cf. 1:26; 2:22; 14:26).

3. Pascal, *Pensées*, 553.

clothes, Gal 3:26–28), of being cleansed from past encumbrances, reborn and renewed (Titus 3:4–7), and of symbolically leaving behind slavery by passing through the Red Sea (1 Cor 10:1–2) and crossing the Jordan to enter the promised land (cf. Mark 1:5). In this context, the sacrament of baptism and its preparation coincided closely with the inner journey of the baptized person.

Things quickly became more complicated. Already in New Testament times, entire households were converted to the new faith (e.g. Acts 16:15; 18:8). And one can conjecture that already in the second generation, for children born into a Christian community, the psychological process of coming to faith was different. By the third century at least, the baptism of infants had become a common practice. And when Christianity became the official religion of the Roman Empire, to be a baptized believer no longer necessarily involved a personal experience of being "grasped by Christ" (Phil 3:12) leading to a change of lifestyle. Following the values they were taught from birth onward, for many centuries people were supposed to live a "good Christian life" as members of a so-called Christian society. These developments meant that the link between baptism and *metanoia*, once evident, became much more tenuous.[4]

At the time of the Reformation, some Christians rediscovered this link and so refused to baptize infants. The Anabaptist movement on the Continent and the Baptists in England conferred baptism only on those who had made a personal choice to be disciples of Christ and consequently could become full and active members of a congregation. For them, baptism was not just the normal entry into Christian society but a radical choice to give one's life to Christ. Today, baptism limited to adults continues in a number of denominations that descend from what is sometimes

---

4. It should be clear that these reflections do not intend to deny the validity of infant baptism, nor the fact that the sacrament, as an initiative of God working through the community of believers, has an efficacy which goes beyond the mere ratification of a human choice. The point at issue here is showing how *metanoia* and its sacramental expression in baptism gradually became separate in time, with the unfortunate result that the significance of both became harder to discern.

called the left wing of the Reformation, although with the passage of time this practice has not always escaped becoming ritualized and stereotyped in its turn. Adult baptism does, however, have the distinct advantage of showing more clearly, along the lines of the New Testament, the link between the sacrament and the inner reorientation of a person's life. This is evident even in the mainstream churches that also practice infant baptism: the renewal of the catechumenate to permit adults to become members of the church—for example the RCIA (Rite for Christian Initiation of Adults) in the Catholic church in the United States—has brought great benefits not just to the newly baptized but to parishes and congregations in general.

It still remains true that for most Christians today, the foundational experience of *metanoia* is not linked in time, and indeed often not even in understanding, to the reception of baptism, nor even to those other key events that in some churches have become part of Christian initiation—confirmation, first communion, solemn profession of faith, etc. It would not be an exaggeration to say that the gap or disconnect between life in Christ and its liturgical expression is one of the greatest obstacles to understanding and living the faith. It results, in the long run, in Christianity being reduced to a "religion," a separate Sunday-morning domain detached from the day-to-day life lived by ordinary women and men. The fact that many people see the practice of the sacraments as things-in-themselves relegated to a separate sphere of existence, and moreover do not view this as a problem, testifies to a serious misconception concerning what the faith in fact is.

There are moments, however, when life and ritual do coincide. In the church today, for example, what the first Christians experienced can come to life through the process by which a woman or man discovers a "religious vocation" and becomes a member of a religious order or congregation. The individual is attracted by the life of an institute or monastery, enters into relationship with it, and undergoes a period of discernment. The purpose of this discernment is not just to see whether they are suited to the religious life, but to allow them to discover that they are invited to say a YES for life to Christ, independent of the particular human characteristics of the community they will join. In fact, such a YES to the person of Christ can be the only efficacious motivation for a commitment of an entire lifetime, because only it comes from the deepest part of a person's being which has been awakened by the call. When a brother of Taizé makes his life-commitment, for example, the prior speaks the following words: "Brother, remember that it is Christ who calls you and that it is to him that you are now going to respond."[5]

For some, ordination to the ministry may be a similar experience of *metanoia*, and for others, marriage. For this to be the case, however, the spouses must discover, in the act of falling in love with another person to the extent that one decides to spend one's entire life with him or her, a love which is not just a human attraction but a being grasped by the Absolute. In this way, marriage becomes a road to respond to Christ, in the community of the family, by the gift of one's existence. Once again, only this can provide a firm foundation for a definitive YES which lasts a lifetime, and it is for this reason that the Catholic Church considers matrimony—like holy orders—a sacrament, since what is called a sacrament is nothing other than the adaptation of baptism to a particular life situation.

In this chapter, then, we have examined the beginning of the process of *metanoia*. It is rooted in an experience that in some sense recapitulates it and sets the framework for one's entire life as a follower of Christ. We can call this a lived experience of baptism, distinct but not separate from the actual celebration of the rite. Ideally, the two are closely connected in time. But whether this is the case or not—and today most often it is not—the celebration of baptism and the entry into *metanoia* are two sides of the same coin. As Saint Paul puts it, we are baptized "into Christ" (Rom 6:3); we take part in his own inner journey through death to life. And since the life of discipleship continues after the lived experience of baptism, therefore *metanoia* does as well. It is to this further stage that we now turn.

5. Roger of Taizé, *Rule*, 121.

CHAPTER 6

Doing God's Will

If we regard *metanoia* not merely as the entry into a life of faith, but as the basic structure of that faith, then it becomes essential to examine the form it takes in the day-to-day life of a believer. A verse from a psalm sets us on the right path:

> Sacrifice and offering you did not desire;
> you have opened my ears.
> Burnt-offering and sin-offering you did not ask for,
> so I said, "Here I am, I am coming!"
> In the scroll of the book it is written of me:
> I delight to do your Will;
> your Law is in the depths of my being
> (Ps 40:6–8)

The author of this ancient prayer already understood that the essential thing was not outward rites or attempts to gain God's favor, but a personal transformation that originates from the side of God. What we earlier referred to as a call is here described as an opening of the ears; God has removed the human obstacles that keep us from hearing a voice that comes from elsewhere. And this awakens in the hearer the spontaneous desire to respond: "Here I am, I am coming!" She then discovers that God's word is not merely something that comes to her from the outside, but rather reveals what was buried in the depths of her being. As a result, her entire life becomes the attempt to walk along that road opened by God, not out of fear or a sense of duty but impelled by a profound and joyful conviction ("delight"). The opening of the ears and the unpremeditated readiness to listen and respond, on the one hand, and the doing of God's will throughout one's lifetime on the other, are two inseparable dimensions of the process of *metanoia*.[1]

But what does it mean to "do God's will"? How do we discover this will and put it into practice? We need to begin by unpacking the expression itself. For many people, the notion of "the will of God" is distasteful or even frightening. It can evoke the image of a deity who has organized everything in advance, leaving human beings in the role of mere marionettes doomed to follow a prearranged course. Or, if some notion of human freedom still persists, it is linked to the idea that unless we figure out, with the limited means at our disposal, what God has already decided we must do, we have missed the boat and are lost for good. This outlook is often coupled with the unsettling suspicion that the inflexible divine will is indifferent or even hostile to our own deepest desires. How often have we heard well-meaning Christians say to a person who has undergone a tragedy, for example someone whose infant daughter has just died of a brain tumor, "I know it's hard, but you just have to accept it as God's will." It is absolutely essential to realize that there is nothing biblical, let alone Christian, about this understanding of the divine will; it undoubtedly comes from some archaic ("pagan") notion of the divinity still rooted deep in our collective unconscious.

It may come as a surprise to learn that the Hebrew word usually employed to designate "God's will" is *ratson*, from the root *rtsh*, "to be delighted, well pleased." The noun *ratson* can therefore be

1. In the Letter to the Hebrews (10:5–7), a version of this psalm is quoted in Greek in which the word "ears" is replaced with "body": "You have prepared a body for me." The Christian author places this verse on the lips of Jesus to illustrate the coming of the Son of God in human form. But if we take "body" in the biblical sense of "presence-in-the-world," it is also relevant to our topic. God makes of us persons capable of discerning and following his will by becoming part of a body prepared for us (see chapter 9).

translated "delight, pleasure, goodwill," in other words it refers to what makes someone happy. So the words of the psalm, "I delight to do your will," can be rendered more precisely "I am happy to do what makes you happy." God's will is not some harsh and rigid commandment that contradicts our deepest desires; it is simply a way of speaking about what God desires for his creation—in a word, *shalom*, life in fullness. And if we love God as the source of our ultimate happiness, we are glad to do what makes God happy. It is not a duty but a source of joy.

It is therefore incorrect to use the expression "God's will" as a synonym for "whatever happens." To say that the death of a child, an epidemic or a war, or any other event that destroys life is God's will would be to say that such a thing makes God happy, and expressed in this way it is clearly a horrible blasphemy. The fact—also testified to in the Scriptures—that God can always find ways to bring good out of evil, that any event, no matter how terrible, can in the final analysis become part of the road towards greater life, is an entirely different question—and that question is answered by the cross.

How are God's desires communicated to human beings? At the beginning of the history of Israel, discerning the will of God was not an individual but rather a collective endeavor. It came through those in charge of the people and was an essential part of their task: first of all Moses and Joshua, followed by those charismatic leaders called the "judges," later on the kings of Israel and, since many of them were not particularly attentive to God, through others called by God for this purpose, those beings of fire we know as the prophets. These inspired men and women attempted to share with their compatriots what they understood as a communication from God. But as time passed, God's will was also set down in writing, notably in the Torah, the first books of our Bible. The Torah speaks of a covenant between God and the people Israel, by which God ensured the protection and well-being of the nation he had chosen. The people, for their part, agreed to live in a certain way by following the stipulations of the covenant, the divine commandments revealed on Mount Sinai. By the time of Jesus, God's will was essentially mediated through a meditation on the sacred books of Israel, our Old Testament, which provided a kind of blueprint for living a life of faithfulness to God, often by means of negative examples. The search to discover God's will was thus open to every reader of the text, though this reading did not occur in isolation but was undertaken with the guidance of educated men, the "experts in the Law," whose role was to teach their fellow Jews how to live in a way pleasing to God.

For Jesus, fully integrated into the history of his people, doing what God wished was the motivating force of his existence. "I have come down from heaven, not to do my will but the will of the one who sent me" (John 6:38; cf. 5:30). And this will, far from being a heavy burden that required an expenditure of energy, was nourishment for him (John 4:34), in other words a source of life. Jesus was deeply rooted in the word of God expressed in the Scriptures, which he spontaneously recognized as his own story. Nonetheless, doing God's will was not for him merely a question of putting a written code into practice. When we read the Gospels, we have the impression that for Jesus, God's will was constantly being revealed in the present moment, through the events and encounters of each new day.

The superficial idea held by some, namely that the man Jesus knew ahead of time all that he was going to do and all that would happen to him, is clearly untenable. One of the most salient characteristics of human beings is their ignorance of the future. If we knew infallibly what the next year, month, week, or hour would bring, our lives would be entirely different. For Jesus to have this knowledge would turn him into a creature totally unlike the rest of us; he would not be "true man" according to the definition of the Council of Chalcedon.

The Jesus we encounter in the Gospels lives totally in God's presence and present, more fully than any other human being. He lets us see that "God's today" is not the empty and meaningless space of someone entirely without past or future; it contains in some sense all of time, since it is rooted in all God has done since the beginning of time and includes the infallible hope of a fulfillment beyond what eye has seen and ear has heard (cf. 1 Cor 2:9). Jesus, unlike the rest of us, is not inhibited by past mistakes or false programming, nor by unrealistic expectations of what is to come; he is neither an optimist nor a pessimist. Jesus is free, in other words fully present to what comes and able to be what his Father wishes him to be at every moment. For him, "doing God's will" means simply living in God's today, without calculation, and thus making God present in the refractory conditions of a world alienated from its Maker.

If we start from this understanding of Jesus's presence, certain gospel stories take on a different appearance. One day, Jesus and his disciples are on the periphery of the land of Israel, and there they encounter a Canaanite woman, a non-Jew, who implores the Master to heal her daughter (Matt 15:21–28). Jesus responds at first by affirming his mission: "I have been sent only to the lost sheep of the house of Israel." When the woman insists, he says some words which appear harsh, but which are in fact simply a restatement and an explanation, in parable form, of the priority of his mission to Israel. "It is not right to take the children's bread and throw it to the puppies." By using the term "dog," habitually used in Jesus's world as an insult, and transforming it into "puppy," Jesus injects a bit of humor and kindness into the situation. The woman, rather than giving up her attempt to get Jesus to help her, replies, "Yes, Lord, but even the puppies eat the crumbs that fall from their masters' table." Her words provoke this response: "O woman, great is your faith! Let it be done to you as you wish." A traditional pious interpretation of this story assumes that Jesus "already" knew what he was going to do and was intentionally testing the woman to elicit her response of trust. If, however, we situate Jesus fully in the present, we see someone who is capable of being surprised. The woman's unexpected behavior calls forth from him words which open up a new understanding of his mission. It would not necessarily follow the expected course found in the biblical books: first a transformation and renewal of all Israel so that subsequently, seeing this, the other nations would turn to God. Strictly speaking, then, should we not say that Jesus does not bring God to those he encounters, as if God were somewhere else, but rather witnesses to and with them to what God is doing here and now? He is the catalyst that opens a closed world to the divine Presence.

What does Jesus's new and unique way of accomplishing God's will mean for us, his followers? Naturally we cannot simply compare ourselves to him. Instead of being totally focused in the present and therefore open to God's will, we are scattered between past and future, often living in regrets and nostalgia on the one hand, and dreams and fears for the future on the other. And even our so-called present existence is, in fact, largely filtered through our notions of what we imagine reality should be, as opposed to what it in fact is. How often, upon meeting someone for the first time, do we not judge him or her in function of all our past encounters? And it is rare that we are surprised by the people and things we know, since we have already classed them in the filing system of our brain. If we are constantly bored and must turn elsewhere to seek new excitement, could this not mean that we have become impermeable to the power of the Real that lies right at our door?

Left to ourselves, then, we are apparently doomed to an inauthentic existence. According to the New Testament, however, Jesus promised his disciples that, after his resurrection, they would continue his work in the world, doing even greater things than he had done (cf. John 14:12). And this would happen, he explained, by the gift of God's own Spirit, the life-force that animated Jesus during his life on earth and that, once risen from the dead, he would bequeath to his followers as a "law" written on their hearts (see Jer 31:33; Ezek 36:26–27). The gift of the Holy Spirit, starting from the first Christian Pentecost (see Acts 2) and continuing throughout history in the act of baptism, thus makes a true *metanoia* possible. It conforms believers to Christ and so enables him to pursue his mission through them. As Saint Paul put it, by baptism we have "put on a new self" (Col 3:10); we are "in Christ" (Rom 8:1; 12:5; 1 Cor 1:30; 2 Cor 5:17: Gal 1:22 etc.) and therefore, in us, Jesus keeps on accomplishing God's will. In a pregnant expression Paul calls Christians "the body of Christ," in other words his ongoing presence in the world. As a result, through our relationship with him, little by little we too become able to live in God's today and to do God's will in the humble circumstances of our lives.

CHAPTER 7

Leaving Our Comfort Zone

*M*etanoia begins by coming to faith in the God of Jesus Christ, expressed in the sacrament of baptism. This beginning, however, is not merely a starting point that is left behind; on the contrary, it determines the basic shape of a believer's existence, the grammar of a Christian's life and activity. Those who pay attention to this communication from beyond their own self are constantly called to discover and do God's will in the particular circumstances of their day-to-day lives, a practice described in the gospels as "following Jesus," in other words walking faithfully in his footsteps. Their life is a life "on the road" in the company of the Son of Man who "has no place to lay his head" (Luke 9:58). It is in this movement forward that they discover the presence of God and allow it to enter and break open a world that ineluctably tends to close itself off in a suicidal complacency.

The first part of the process is a leaving behind. "Go from your land and your kindred and your father's house" were the first words addressed by God to Abraham on the threshold of the Biblical narrative (Gen 12:1). For the patriarch, this injunction had a very concrete meaning, just as it did for the first disciples of Jesus. Over the centuries, as a result of the choice to follow Christ, multitudes of people have experienced a literal break with their background—their families, friends, and the values that formed them. They were easily able to make their own Saint Paul's affirmation: "I consider everything a disadvantage because of what is far superior—knowing Christ Jesus my Lord. For him I have lost everything, and consider it rubbish" (Phil 3:8).

But once this break is made, or if there has been no actual departure, how does one go on living this dimension of *metanoia*? What does it mean to leave home as a daily practice? A good way to answer these questions is to analyze an expression that has become current in recent years: the *comfort zone*.

It has often been said that human beings, in comparison with most other animal species, are born particularly incomplete. We are not hard-wired with instincts that clearly define our behavior once and for all. A human child, through interaction with the environment and the persons around him or her, has slowly to learn a style of being, expectations, and strategies for coping with the challenges presented by life. We can call this process the development of a *self*.[1] When it is successful, the individual has acquired an identity which gives a profound feeling of security and the courage to confront the unknown. When the formation of the self is not successful, however, perhaps because of a particularly threatening environment or an inadequate upbringing, a person is handicapped on their life journey; they are forced to spend a lot of time and energy trying to make up for the deficiencies in their ability to relate to the world. Naturally most of us are situated somewhere in the middle, with a self "good enough" to withstand the ordinary stresses of life, whereas at certain moments we are overwhelmed and react poorly. In any event, life always sets new challenges before us, so that the self is never a finished product but rather reforms itself in a series of stages we grow.

When our self is functional, we feel secure and comfortable. What we know and the habits that define our behavior give us a sense that we are in control of our environment. We have a home, a nest, and this is what people often refer to as a "comfort zone"—the

---

1. Although certain psychological theories distinguish between a more superficial *ego* and a deeper *self*, this is not relevant to our reflections here.

place where life makes sense and where all seems right with the world.

This necessary basis for human functioning, however, has another aspect. Life is infinitely greater than our understanding of it, and so our comfort zone necessarily involves a restriction of reality. A lot is left out, and what is allowed in is often distorted to fit the needs of the individual at a given moment in time. We are limited by the prejudices of our tribe, by our own deep unwillingness to confront things that disturb our equilibrium, and simply by aspects of reality we have not yet encountered. Fortunately or not, reality tends inevitably to break in and "disturb" us, calling into question what we have attained, in an often painful process of readaptation. As the Harvard psychologist Robert Kegan puts it, the human journey is a series of "evolutionary truces," whereby we forge a stable self that functions for a time, until it is rendered problematic by new inner or outer events. This crisis leads to a breakdown, which eventually culminates in another period of stability, and the process begins all over again.[2] The psychological health of a person can be judged by his or her ability to deal with the inevitable crises that occur, letting go of old habits and convictions to allow new elements to be integrated into the self. A significant part of what we call mental illness consists in clinging to old strategies of adaptation that once were useful but no longer work in one's current environment.

If we relate our topic to the understanding of human life we have just examined, it should be clear that, even for those who remain at home physically, *metanoia* necessarily involves the call to leave one's comfort zone to set out into the unknown in the company of Christ. This does not mean systematically rejecting all of one's learned behavior and past achievements, an impossible and indeed inhuman task. The problem is not the self, but the clinging, the fear to open oneself to the new. To express it in other terms, Comfort and Security are good spirits that can accompany us on our journey through life, but contemporary society has made

2. Kegan, *Evolving Self*. I have discussed this model in my book *Life on the Edge*, 168–172.

them into gods, and therefore idols, which take the place of the living God and, in the end, asphyxiate us. It is for that reason that God, who wants only what is best for us, can only reach many of our contemporaries through the paradoxical language of the misfortunes that they suffer, the devastating power of which is directly proportional to the strength of resistance of the bastions they have built around their individual and collective selves. The wall has to be breached come what may, so that life can circulate once again. "He sends out his word and melts them; he makes his wind blow and the waters flow" (Ps 147:18).[3]

Misfortunes that shake the foundations of our personal and social compromises offer the opportunity of discovering a deeper and truer life, but they do not of themselves achieve this. What must also occur is that, in the heart of the adversity, a trust be born that allows us to see that what appeared to be an ending was, in fact, the possibility of a new beginning. For the followers of Jesus, this trust comes from their relationship to the One who walks with them in the dark valley, the One who has already passed through death and vanquished it, and it is his presence that inspires in them the courage and the strength to head into the unknown. They realize that the meaning of their existence is not found in what they already know and have attained, but in allowing themselves to be led, beyond their achievements, to new lands in which God is waiting to meet them.

If clinging to what one has acquired is the main obstacle to discovering and doing the will of God, then it follows that *metanoia* involves learning a certain detachment. Not in the sense that we consider persons and things as unimportant—detachment is not indifference—but that we see them as gifts that do not belong to us and that we cannot simply use as we wish. This detachment is not easy to achieve, even for those whose desire to respond to the call is strong. Fear of the unknown and the comforts of a world made in our image are powerful impulses that inhibit our journey in the steps of Christ. Happily, God has provided remedies for our

3. This follows from an examination of the theme of "God's anger" in the Bible. See John of Taizé, *Wrath*.

weakness. We are not simply asked to follow the invisible Christ blindly, all by ourselves. Others are walking with us on this road, and many who have gone before us show us the way. First of all, we can find support in the earthly life of Jesus and his first disciples that we encounter in the pages of the New Testament, and in the example of believers from the beginning down to the present day. Personally, I had the not, always, comfortable privilege of living for thirty years with a man, Brother Roger of Taizé, whose daily question was "What is Christ asking of us today?" and whose life was the polar opposite of nostalgia or complacency. When we find our place as part of this "cloud of witnesses" (Heb 12:1), we can set out with confidence on this road of nonconformity to the lifestyle of the majority, knowing that we are not alone. By its very nature, *metanoia* has a communal dimension.

Another essential means of achieving detachment is the practice of prayer. Although prayer can take many forms, by definition it means placing ourselves consciously in the presence of God. It thus involves shifting our center of gravity from our own personal drama to "the things above" (Col 3:1), and in this way actualizing the meaning of faith. When our prayer involves times of silence, where slowly those obsessive inner voices quiet down and are seen as relative, we become more capable of openness to the present. This gives us the capacity to discern, in the events of each moment, where we are being led. We are given eyes to see a path—or more exactly the next steps to take—where before all seemed opaque and confused.

Metanoia thus involves the discovery that we discern and do God's will, not by remaining stuck in the comfort zone of our settled convictions and habits, but by the lure of the uncharted land beyond, what Pope Francis calls the peripheries of life. What makes this departure possible is the knowledge that, in leaving home like Abraham, we are not alone; Christ has gone before us and remains with us on this road. And then, a final transformation can take place. Whereas at first we cross the threshold of our self and take timid steps out of our door, trusting in Christ but ready to scurry back home at the first sign of danger, gradually we acquire a taste for the pilgrim's life and learn to feel more at home with the risen Jesus on the road than with the illusory comforts of a settled life. Jesus himself has become our comfort zone, and so we have fulfilled Georg Simmel's definition of an adventurer, the person who "makes a system of life out of life's lack of system."

CHAPTER 8

Illusions, Ideologies, and Information

A t this point it is time to examine more in detail the intellectual component of *metanoia*. Of all the animal species,
homo sapiens is the only one endowed with the capacity to reason.
Despite the tendency in recent times to see human beings as just
another animal species, the very fact that I can make these marks
on a computer screen or a page, and that you can look at them perhaps years later and respond, not to the marks themselves but to a
whole implicit world accessible to you through them, immediately
distinguishes us even from such evolved animals as chimpanzees
and dolphins. What is being described here is obviously the fact
of human language, the symbol-making capacity of the human
species.[1]

A simple way to grasp this evolutionary advance is to make a
distinction between signs and symbols. Animals respond to *signs*,
which point to the presence, or imminent presence, of a reality de-
sired or feared. Humans, in addition to this, employ *symbols*, most
usually words, which enable them to construct a virtual universe

---

1. The classic study of this topic is Langer, *Philosophy in a New Key.* For a
more detailed application of the theory of symbolism to language see Percy,
Message in the Bottle.

they can share with others. To say "Mother" or "Abraham Lincoln" or "Santa Claus" is not necessarily to announce the arrival of a certain individual, but more often to evoke a being with an entire history, a being who may not even exist any longer as a material entity, or who may never have existed as such. In fact, we spend most of our time in this virtual universe—the source of our likes and dislikes, the basis for our choices. To put it another way, we live in a world mediated by meaning, a world of symbols and not just of objects.

In order to live and to act, human beings thus have a compelling need to find meaning. They need to see their existence as part of a story possessing a logic and a direction, a guiding narrative which enables them to "make sense" of the data with which they are constantly assailed. Such a story takes the multifarious events of existence and weaves them into a worldview that allows a person to interpret these events and consequently to orient his or her life in a certain way. Since, in a rationalistic age, the word "myth" has become ambiguous and for many people simply means a false explanation of reality, let us refer to this overarching story as a *mythos*.

A mythos is not something we invent by ourselves out of nothing. It comes largely from the human society into which we are born, and indeed gives that society its particular physiognomy. It defines to a great extent the identity of its members and their understanding of life. It enables them to decide, for example, whether certain other people or groups are friends to be welcomed or enemies to be feared or combated. It tells them whether a certain way of dressing is acceptable or not, whether this or that occupation is honorable or disreputable, and so on. Although the basic structure of a mythos is unchanging, it is not simply a static reality. The health of a civilization, like that of an individual, depends in large part on its ability to integrate new factors that arise.

The mythos of small traditional societies was all-encompassing and shared by almost all the members. In more complex societies, people sometimes have to negotiate between various mythoi; they are torn for instance between their duty to their family or religion and to their nation. In our highly fragmented contemporary world, where hundreds of larger and smaller narratives compete for our attention, most people are forced to patch together a personal mythos out of elements taken from a multitude of sources, sometimes barely compatible among themselves. This work of personal mythos-making is precarious and often a cause of anxiety; human beings are simply not meant to reinvent the universe all alone.

A general unease thus permeates our world today, with the specter of meaninglessness constantly threatening our most impressive achievements. At the time of the First World War, the German poet Rainer Maria Rilke had already grasped that "the astute animals themselves note that we are not completely at home in our interpreted world."[2] This anxiety causes some to turn to fanaticism, a hermetic worldview shared by a small group of like-minded souls that claims to give infallible answers to all the questions of existence and consigns all others to the outer darkness. Another more common solution is simply to abandon the quest for a global meaning, remaining on the surface of life and focusing on immediate pleasures and the avoidance of all discomfort. Such an outlook, paradoxically, leaves us less free because we are less able to make intelligent and meaningful choices. With no rational mythos to orient our behavior, we are more subject to manipulation by a technocratic society with its purely utilitarian norms and goals.

In the past, this search for life's meaning gave rise to religions and then, concomitant with the secularization of societies, to ideologies that provided an apparently workable mythos for collective life without invoking the notion of the divine. Today we have taken a further step. The implicit mythos that undergirds a globalized neoliberal society has very little intellectual content and is rooted in lower-level values such as comfort, security, and pleasure, and the maintenance of power and privilege for those already possessing them. It is based on the primacy of economic and

2. Die findigen Tiere merken es schon, | daß wir nicht sehr verläßlich zu Haus sind | in der gedeuteten Welt (Rilke, *Duino Elegies* 1; my translation).

technological criteria, rather than what used to be considered the higher realms of the human spirit.[3] Individuals and groups may of course choose to opt out of this worldview, and many do so, but since it is largely unformulated, in other words not based on an explicit mythos such as Christian or Marxist doctrine but incarnate in the institutions of our societies, everyone is influenced by it in a host of subtle ways, regardless of their conscious choices. In spite of the appearance of diversity, it must be admitted that expressing true dissent and finding true alternatives in our day is just as arduous as it has ever been, if not more so.

The mythoi of the small and great civilizations that have arisen across the centuries contain a host of treasures, the result of human ingenuity in the face of an enormous variety of situations. At the same time, it is of the utmost importance to realize that human mythoi inevitably have their blind spots and limitations; they are never simply a map of the world as it truly is. This is the ineluctable disadvantage of the incomparable symbol-making ability of our species. We can—and indeed must—create a virtual universe to orient our understanding and behavior, and this allows us to achieve a mastery over creation of which no other living species is capable. But this virtual universe, enshrined in a mythos, is not only incomplete, but fatally flawed. It involves an inevitable portion of illusion, due notably to its rootedness in a particular society, group or individual. We see things from our own point of view, which is both limited and biased. Conflicts arise in human history not only over the possession of goods and resources, as is the case with animal species, but more specifically over disagreements about the mythoi which justify each actor's claims. Whether it is a question of a brother and sister quarreling over an inheritance, political parties offering solutions to the ills of society, or entire nations going to war because their way of life seems threatened, our actions are conditioned by an implicit or explicit mythos assuring us that we are right and our adversary is wrong.

3. For a more detailed account see John of Taizé, *Life on the Edge*, 172–78. See also the encyclical of Pope Francis, *Laudato Si'*, particularly chapter III.

In this context, how is it possible to live a Christian life? The early followers of Jesus, those we encounter in the pages of the New Testament, belonged to small intensive communities animated by a mythos radically different from the world around them. This mythos came to them from the Hebrew Scriptures and told the story of a particular people, Israel, brought into being and sustained by the actions of a God unlike any other, then transfigured and widened to include all humanity through the teaching of the Messiah, Jesus of Nazareth. This story continued to inspire and motivate the members of the community not just through their human memory and understanding—although meditation on the Scriptural sources has always been an essential part of the life of faith—but by the active presence of God's Spirit, bestowed upon them by the Risen Christ, which kept alive the outlook of Jesus and led believers ever further into the truth about existence (see John 14:26; 16:13).

What could thus seem, viewed from the outside, to be just one mythos among many was revealed to be, by those who took the risk of trusting in the messenger from God, a message that radically challenged all human understanding. The process of *metanoia* consequently involves a calling into question of all those self-justifications by which we project our own limited outlook onto the universe. It takes us out of what Saint John calls "the world," a circumscribed and self-centered worldview, and changes our perspective, allowing us to see things more and more, so to speak, with the eyes of God.[4]

This process is known in the Bible as the acquisition of *wisdom*. Already in the Hebrew Scriptures, wisdom is not viewed as gaining some sort of theoretical or abstract knowledge but as the

4. In our day, the fact that the Absolute is revealed in the contingency of history is one of the greatest stumbling-blocks to faith in Christ. Is this not, to a great extent, an (over-)reaction to the error of triumphalism we examined earlier and to the general human tendency to absolutize one's own mythos? See also p. 23, note 2. This does not mean, on the other hand, that all the details of the Christian mythos are definitive and infallible. An understanding of the faith evolves across the centuries and a process of reinterpretation is an essential part of this.

answer to the questions "What is the good life?" and "How does one live it?" In the New Testament, true wisdom is distinguished from mere human cleverness or erudition (cf. Col 2:8; 2 Tim 2:14) and the arts of persuasion (cf. Col 2:4), qualities which taken in themselves lead only to arrogance (1 Cor 8:1–2) and disputes (1 Tim 6:4; Jas 3:13–18). Wisdom is fundamentally a divine gift, an inspiration from above (2 Cor 1:12; Eph 1:17; Jas 1:5). Saint John, possibly alluding to baptism, describes it as the result of an "anointing from the Holy One," which imparts to us the truth about God and the world (1 John 2:20–21, 27). For Paul wisdom is a fruit of the Spirit (1 Cor 2:7–15) that gives us "the mind of Christ" (1 Cor 2:16) and reveals to us "the mystery of Christ" (Eph 3:3–4; Col 2:2–3), in other words the direction and purpose of creation and history as seen from God's overarching perspective.

Naturally, this change of perspective does not occur in a flash; it is an ongoing and endless process of reinterpretation and deepening, since God's ways are infinite. Although this process has an intellectual component, it is not a theory about existence but rather the capacity to exercise discernment. As Saint Paul writes to the Philippians:

> This is my prayer: that your love may increase more and
> more in understanding and every sort of perceptiveness,
> so that you can discern what is most appropriate. (Phil
> 1:9–10a)

Today we tend to think of love as a feeling or emotion, something distinct from understanding. But according to Paul, God's love communicated to us, which turns us into women and men capable of loving, enables us at the same time to discern how God asks us to live out this love in the concrete situations of our lives (cf. also Heb 5:14). Along the same lines, the apostle counsels the Christians of Rome:

> Do not be conformed to this age, but be transformed by
> the renewing of your minds so as to be able to discern
> what is the will of God, what is good and suitable and
> perfect. (Rom 12:2)

Metanoia thus involves a continuous renewal of our understanding (cf. Eph 4:23; Col 3:10), which eliminates one by one the obstacles to living fully as true disciples in God's today.

It is certainly the case that, in our day, most Christians do not live surrounded by like-minded people. Rather, they generally attempt to practice their faith in the midst of a society with quite different priorities, where mythoi of all sorts compete for their allegiance. The work of intellectual conversion is thus more arduous than ever; it goes far beyond recognizing and rejecting obvious moral evils. It aims at the acquisition of a critical perspective on reality that is antithetical to many of the "truths" that people immersed in their own mythos take for granted. It makes believers, often against their conscious intention, into people who go against the stream.

Metanoia thus involves a gradual unmasking of the illusions by which the mass of people orient their lives. That the worth of a person, for example, is determined by his or her prestige or achievements. That wealth and power are keys to happiness. That freedom means having the right to do whatever I want. That I am justified in placing my own concerns before those of others. That sex is an activity purely at the disposition of human beings and exists basically to give them pleasure. That the will of the majority infallibly tells us what is right and worthwhile. That science is the most certain and fullest source of truth, and thus there is no real reason not to do whatever it tells us we can do. That human beings have the right to exploit the earth and all it contains for their own ends. That security is always to be preferred to taking risks. That I deserve whatever I have attained by my own efforts. That being realistic means compromising my deepest convictions when necessary.

Such a catalogue, admittedly only a rough guide, could be prolonged indefinitely, adapted to different situations and applied to all the dimensions of life, from personal relationships to the organization of local and global society. When illusions of this sort are seen through, a space opens up where we can discern in every situation how God is at work in the world, often in ways that are highly disconcerting to those who cling to the understanding of reality they have received from their culture. This long-term work of detoxification is certainly not easy, but it is the source of a deep joy and freedom. Was this not what Saint Paul was explaining to the Christians of Thessalonica? He wrote to them, "You have turned to God from idols, to serve the living and true God" (1 Thess 1:9).

Metanoia is, in particular, a profoundly anti-ideological stance. An ideology is by definition a mythos that claims to offer a total explanation of reality based on uniquely human criteria, which are seen as hard-and-fast laws. The classic example of this is Marxism, where everything is viewed through the lens of economic relationships and class struggle. After the breakup of the communist world in 1989, some were led to speak of the end of ideology. Unfortunately, ideologies are still very much with us today, although in a far less explicit and unequivocal fashion than before. Neoliberal economics and what Pope Francis calls "the technocratic paradigm"[5] determine the behavior of individuals and the priorities of a globalizing society in a multitude of ways.

Although the world he lived in was very different from ours, Saint Paul's reflections on "the Law," especially in his letters to the Galatians and the Romans, offer a firm basis for a critique of ideology from the standpoint of the Christian faith. What the apostle calls in Greek *ho nomos*, "the Law," is in fact the Torah, the divine teaching revealed by God through Moses on Mount Sinai and codified in the biblical books. It is thus not a secular ideology or a rigid blueprint we are constrained to follow blindly, but a privileged expression of the way God wishes people to live: "the Law is holy and the commandment is holy and just and good" (Rom 7:12).

And yet this reality, excellent in itself, became an obstacle to the discovery of the living God, insofar as it was seen as an end and not a means—the source of life and truth and not a pointer to a Presence which remained elusive. People could become complacent that they possessed all the answers, and therefore shut their eyes to what God was doing right in front of their noses.

5. Francis, *Laudato Si'*, §106–14.

Paradoxically, the divine teaching could become a motive for self-justification, the failure to be open to the unsettling will of God revealed in the here-and-now.

Paul's criticism of the Law applies to an even greater degree to any view of reality rooted in concepts already acquired and possessed, instead of in receptivity to a dimension that transcends human making and doing, the capacity to welcome and discern what comes to us from elsewhere. In more specifically biblical and Christian terms, it has to do with a failure to see life as the ongoing gift of God, accessible to our understanding and transformed into wisdom if and when we let go of our preconceptions and self-centered judgments. *Metanoia* is precisely this capacity to let go, to accept that it is often by our unknowing that we attain a deeper and truer knowledge, one that does not belong to us. An ideological view of the world, on the contrary, leads to a judgmental attitude and the rejection of all that does not fit into its scheme of things. It inevitably veers towards moralism, insofar as it divides the world into those who follow the straight and narrow path and those who do not, and in addition leaves no room for forgiveness. It eradicates joy. When the justification for this comes from religious motives, as it sometimes does, the error is even deeper, because this places a veneer of the infinite over a this-worldly and self-centered endeavor. By identifying itself with absolute truth that is implicitly considered a possession, such an attitude is in the final analysis a form of idolatry. It confuses the Spirit of the living God with a code set in stone once and for all and permanently at the disposition of true believers.

The world of today has traveled still further along the road of the flight from wisdom, in an infinitely more insidious manner. The virtual world we have created is no longer translated into an ideology expressed in words to which we are required to adhere; technology has incarnated this worldview in hardware and software without which it is almost impossible to live together with others. Moreover, this digital society of ours is based on postulates that evacuate any transcendent dimension out of hand. When words and symbols are treated as mere information, counters that can be manipulated at will by ever more powerful machines, the question of meaning is at best taken for granted but more often bypassed. What is called intelligence, artificial by nature, is reduced to the game of rearranging these bits of information as quickly and efficiently as possible. No wonder that some have begun to speak of a "content problem": we are getting better and better at packaging the material that is given to us, but in the final analysis where does it come from, and what is its significance? Such questions are off the radar screen of contemporary culture's way of proceeding. Mesmerized by all the "special effects," caught in the web of the easy and often rather mindless communication of social media, we have less and less time and inclination to ask where in fact we are heading. The new laws that condition our understanding of reality are not the divine commandments, but the algorithms of our virtual universe. One of the great questions of today is thus whether it is possible to tame technological progress, placing it at the service of an authentically human life that maintains an openness to the Absolute, or whether it will lead to what some have called the end of the human race, asphyxiated by the works of our own hands.

Illusions, ideologies, information: all of this represents a formidable barrier to discerning the will of God in the present moment. On the level of the intellect, *metanoia* is thus the gradual process of becoming aware of the negative side of our prodigious symbol-making capacity and finding a way out. This is made possible above all by a life of contemplative prayer. In the silence of prayer, our hearts and minds are awakened to the Other who is revealed beyond all our inner chatter and clutter. As our inner operations quiet down, we become more attuned to the working of God's Spirit within us and in the world around us. Our perception is cleansed and our outlook simplified. The center of gravity slowly passes from the head to the heart, and even to the body. Virtual reality gradually gives way to a perception of the Real. The fog lifts and we begin to grasp, at first only in fits and starts, "what eye has not seen and ear has not heard, what has never arisen in the human heart: the things God has prepared for those who love him" (1 Cor 2:9).

CHAPTER 9

Discerning the Body

The *metanoia* of the intellect clearly has as its goal not simply to purify our minds, but rather to make possible a different way of being in the world. As Jesus points out in one of his parables, the wise man is one who builds his house on rock (see Matt 7:24). It should be obvious that the earlier criticism of moralism was in no way meant to minimize the importance of human activity. The error of moralism is simply that it intervenes too late in the process: it attempts to change behavior by means of prescriptions and admonitions, without examining the roots of that behavior in a particular stance towards the world. Jesus tells us, on the contrary, that we cannot hope to get good fruit from a diseased tree. When the tree is healthy, the fruit will necessarily be whole (cf. Luke 6:43–44). Doing follows from being, and for humans this is rooted in what Jesus calls the heart, the true me, the core of the personality. So he continues:

> The good person brings forth good things from the good treasure-chest of his heart, and the evil person brings forth evil from his evil treasure. (Luke 6:45)

To the extent that our outlook is healed and transformed by the activity of God's Spirit, our actions will be more in harmony with God's wishes; we will exercise a positive influence on the people and on the world around us. And we will do so without being forced to act in a way contrary to our deepest impulses, a procedure which in the end leads only to play-acting, to the hypocrisy so strongly condemned by Jesus.

Here we can glimpse what is problematic about the customary fashion in which morality has been presented in the Christian world. By emphasizing above all the rejection of evil and an obsession with sin, moralists run the great risk of motivating people to seek a surface conformity that simply covers up the shadow-side of human beings. The only road to authentic behavior is to become aware of all that is in us and to open it to God's beneficial and wonder-working light. Neither scrupulosity (the flight from the unmentionable) nor licentiousness (the return of the repressed) offer a solution to the problem of human activity, but only a basic trust in the One who loves us in spite of our refusals and who thus gives us the courage to face them and to look beyond.

Let us now attempt to describe the basic stance resulting from the process of *metanoia* that leads to a life according to the Gospel, to forms of activity that make God present in our world. A good place to begin is with two texts from Saint Paul:

> [Christ] died for all, so that the living no longer live for themselves but for the one who died and rose for them. (2 Cor 5:15)

> None of us lives for ourselves and dies for ourselves. For if we live, we live for the Lord, if we die, we die for the Lord; so whether we live or die, we belong to the Lord. For that is why Christ died and lived—to be Lord of the dead and the living. (Rom 14:7-9)

In these passages, the apostle describes the decisive change that comes about in people through the death and resurrection of Christ as a shift in *belonging*. Those who take the gospel message to heart and turn to Christ realize that henceforth they no longer belong to themselves but to him (cf. also Gal 3:29; 1 Cor 15:23). This change goes much further than simply putting into practice the teachings of a spiritual master or following certain rules of behavior. It deals not with actions but with a person's basic identity. Such a person no longer possesses herself fully; she has let go and surrendered control of her own being to become part of something infinitely larger.

It must be admitted that the notion of living to or for oneself, of belonging to oneself, has a certain attraction and it is not easily relinquished. To many people autonomy, literally being a law unto oneself, appears to be one of the essential aspects of a fully human existence. This is truer than ever in our world today where, for centuries now, the mythos of the Western world, which is becoming more and more globalized, has exercised a deep fascination, and this mythos has individualism as one of its key tenets. It has led us to see ourselves as detached individuals, independent beings whose happiness consists in the freedom to determine our own existence, liberated from all external constraints. Is it not fair to say that people today aspire above all to "do their own thing," and consider any limits to their choices as an intolerable imposition?

Naturally, like all people immersed in their own mythos, we are largely unaware of the substantial part of illusion that it involves. First of all, none of us are fully autonomous: our vision of the world, our values and priorities, have been largely determined by our background, by the people and events who have contributed to the formation of our character. Whether we like it or not, we carry around within ourselves the entire history of our families, our country, and our world. Moreover, our freedom in the present is curtailed by a society which enforces conformity to an arguably unprecedented degree, both through mass propaganda (the corporate and social media) and through positive laws, often dictated by fear.[1] As in the famous novel by George Orwell, *1984*, talking

1. Patrick Deneen, in his groundbreaking work *Why Liberalism Failed*, brilliantly describes how liberal political theory reduces social reality to two actors, the isolated individual and the State, with a corresponding inflation of the role of law. "Under liberalism, human beings increasingly live in a condition of autonomy in which the threatened anarchy of our purportedly natural condition is controlled and suppressed through the imposition of laws and the corresponding growth of the state. . . . Ironically, the more completely the sphere of autonomy is secured, the more comprehensive the state must

screens (and earphones) are omnipresent. And were someone from another age to come back to earth and observe the lines of people in airports, ordinary citizens innocent of any wrongdoing, submitting passively to the most invasive examinations of their possessions and their persons, they would undoubtedly conclude that they were slaves or prisoners at the mercy of their masters.[2]

In addition, the claim to autonomy brings with it its own anxieties. It requires us essentially to reinvent the universe, elaborating a philosophy of life with no ultimate justification outside of personal taste. If I can do or be anything in theory, how in fact am I to know what I should do or be? Freedom is empty, and ultimately destructive, without guidelines for its exercise, without an orientation that come from some source outside the self. For this reason, it is not uncommon to see men and women suddenly flip from a self-centered and directionless life to membership in a closed group that henceforth controls all the aspects of their personality. The prospect of unrestricted independence was simply too much for them to bear.

In any event, the idea of no longer belonging to oneself is not at first sight appealing. It is essentially the way that the ancient world would have defined slaves as opposed to free citizens. So it is not for nothing that Saint Paul, for example, willingly describes himself as "a slave of Christ" (Rom 1:1; Gal 1:10; Phil 1:1). Many of our translations have watered this down to "servant," but the Greek word *doulos* refers unambiguously to the social status of a slave, someone required to follow the dictates of a master and bereft of the freedom to follow his or her own inclinations. That is also why Paul can describe baptism, the choice to follow Christ as a member

---

become. . . . With the liberation of individuals from [associations and relationships], there is more need to regulate behavior through the imposition of positive law" (38). Seen from another angle, this corresponds to the waning in political life of legitimacy as opposed to legality, of justice as opposed to law. See Agamben, *Mystery of Evil*.

2. After this book was written the world experienced the pandemic of COVID-19, which vastly heightened the reign of fear and the concomitant expansion of the role of public authorities and the influence of "experts" on people's lives.

of the Christian community, as a death to one's previous life—and indeed to one's former self (cf. Rom 6:3).

This death, however, is not something pernicious, for in fact it is not a dead-end but, paradoxically, the transition to a far better state of affairs:

> We have been buried with Christ through baptism into death so that, just as Christ was raised from the dead by the glory of the Father, we too should walk in newness of life. (Rom 6:4)

The risen Jesus is not a harsh taskmaster alienating us by robbing us of our freedom of action, but the Son of God in whom we were created (John 1:3; Col 1:16). As a result, he knows us better than we know ourselves. Belonging to him thus means discovering our true identity, unlimited vistas far beyond what we could have ever imagined. *Metanoia* is the process of casting off the chains of an illusory autonomy, which is in fact a captivity in the prison of one's self and bondage to the values of a world doomed to disappear (see Col 2:8; Eph 2:1–3; 4:22–24). It allows us to emerge from a stagnant pool of water into the great flow of the divine life (cf. Jer 2:13). To be a slave of Christ means, in the final analysis, to reign together with him (see 2 Tim 2:12; Rev 5:10; 22:5).

One of the key truths revealed in the New Testament is the unity of two loves—love of God and love of neighbor. "The person who does not love the brother or sister they see is incapable of loving the God they have not seen," Saint John tells us (1 John 4:20). Analogously, if our new identity is found in Christ, we are somehow linked by that to all those who belong to him. In the writings of Saint Paul, this truth is expressed in exemplary fashion by the image of the *body*.

The Anglican bishop and Bible scholar John A. T. Robinson is the one who dealt with this topic most extensively.[3] He viewed the body as the central concept that unified Paul's thought. He pointed out in the first place that, for the Semitic mentality and unlike the Greek, *basar*—which can be translated as both "flesh"

---

3. See his book *The Body*.

and "body"—is not the mere envelope of the true self, nor what
separates one person from another:

> The flesh-body was not what partitioned a man off from
> his neighbour; it was rather what bound him in the bun-
> dle of life with all men and nature, so that he could never
> make his unique answer to God as an isolated individual,
> apart from his relation to his neighbor. The *basar* contin-
> ued, even in the age of greater religious individualism, to
> represent the fact that personality is essentially social.[4]

Basar is not one component of our being, but rather the
whole human being seen in its solidarity with the rest of creation.
Paul, for his part, goes a step further. Writing in Greek, he distinguishes between the two terms "flesh" (*sarx*) and "body" (*sōma*).
He generally uses the word "flesh" to refer to human beings insofar as they are part and parcel of the present human condition,
marked by alienation from the Source of their being. It thus tends
to have a negative connotation in his thought: "Those who are in
the flesh cannot please God. . . . Flesh and blood cannot inherit
the Kingdom of God" (Rom 8:8; 1 Cor 15:50). The term "body,"
on the other hand, although it retains many of the same meanings
as "the flesh," is used by the apostle to describe a more permanent
dimension of human existence: "While *sarx* stands for man, in the
solidarity of creation, in his distance from God, *sôma* stands for
man, in the solidarity of creation, as made for God."[5] Salvation,
for Paul and indeed for the entire New Testament, thus consists
not in the separation of a perishable body from an immortal soul,
but rather in "the redemption of our body" (Rom 8:23), which is
equivalent to its resurrection from the dead, because "the body is
for the Lord, and the Lord for the body" (1 Cor 6:13).

By entering bodily into our human condition ("in the likeness
of flesh marked by sin," Rom 8:3), going to its lowest point in an
atrocious death (cf. Phil 2:8), and then rising from the dead, Jesus
fundamentally changed that condition. He eliminated in himself
its noxious dimension, its aspect of refusing God in the name of an

4. Robinson, *Body*, 15.
5. Robinson, *Body*, 31.

illusory self-sufficiency, and turned this condition into pure communion. And the very same transformation is offered to us:

> The Lord Jesus Christ will transfigure our lowly body to conform it to the body of his glory, by the power through which he is able to subject all things to himself. (Phil 3:21)

Although here Paul describes this passage as a future event, in fact it has already begun in us through baptism, when we die with Christ to enter a new life. And at this point we come to another use of the term "body," one which has usually not been seen in connection with the foregoing considerations: we enter this new life in no other way than by becoming part of "the body of Christ," which takes shape as a visible, historical reality in the community of believers, the church.

We have become accustomed to using the term "body" to refer, as one dictionary puts it, to "a group of persons associated by some common tie or occupation and regarded as an entity." We thus generally take the expression "the body of Christ" as a simple metaphor for the church as a social institution, and completely miss the breathtaking realism of Paul's thinking in this matter. For him, the community of believers is literally Christ's body or, to put it another way, the continuation of the Messiah's presence in human history. This discovery was in fact the fundamental experience that led the former Pharisee to become a disciple of Jesus:

> As he was on the road approaching Damascus, suddenly a light from heaven shone around him. As he fell to the ground he heard a voice say to him, "Saul, Saul, why are you persecuting me?" "Who are you, Lord?" he replied. "I am Jesus, the one you are persecuting." (Acts 9:3–5)

All at once, Paul realizes that Jesus is indeed alive and, through the life of his followers, still present and active in the world.

"There is one body" (Eph 4:4). Impossible as it is for us to imagine, the body of Christ that is the church is the very same body that hung on the cross and rose from the dead. Perhaps an approach to this truth can come from the realization that when the

Son of God became a human being, he united himself not just to one individual but assumed the human condition in its entirety,[6] and thus became a point of crystallization for a renewed humanity and indeed a renewed creation.

And now we come to a third use of the word "body," which is likewise not separate from the other two but refers to the very same reality—the body of Christ in which believers partake during the celebration of the Lord's Supper, the Eucharist.

> The cup of blessing that we bless, is it not a sharing in the blood of Christ? The bread that we break, is it not a sharing in the body of Christ? Since there is one loaf of bread, we, many as we are, are one body, for we partake in the one bread. (1 Cor 10:16–17)

The realism of Paul's comprehension of this threefold body is shown dramatically in a delicate situation of a Christian community in Corinth with which he attempts to deal. When the believers gather for their weekly assembly, presumably in the home of a well-to-do family, those who are of the same social class as their hosts have the leisure to arrive early, be welcomed into the dining-room, and partake of the delicacies prepared for the guests. The poorer members of the community, on the other hand, notably the slaves, are required to work all day and thus can only arrive at the last minute; they are shown into the patio and forced to be content with any leftovers that remain. When all are present, the person in charge of the community repeats Jesus's words at the Last Supper over the bread and wine, which are then shared among all (see 1 Cor 11:17–22).

Such a scenario would have been considered normal at a typical Greek or Roman gathering, where class differences were taken for granted. Paul, however, wants his hearers to realize that, for the followers of Jesus, this is an unacceptable and indeed shocking state of affairs. And to explain why the lack of material sharing

6. In this respect, the founder of Taizé liked to repeat the phrase of *Gaudium et spes*, 22, quoted by Pope John Paul II in his first encyclical *Redemptor hominis*, 8: "For by His incarnation the Son of God has united Himself in some fashion with every man."

makes their celebration of the Eucharist a sham, the apostle employs the image of the body:

> If someone eats the bread and drinks the cup of the Lord unworthily, that person is guilty of the body and blood of the Lord. . . . For they eat and drink judgment upon themselves by eating and drinking without discerning the body. (1 Cor 11:27, 29)

Receiving the Eucharist in an unworthy or sacrilegious manner is equivalent here to receiving it "without discerning the body." Many commentators across the centuries, projecting a later theology on to the letters of Paul, imagined that the apostle was criticizing the incapacity or unwillingness to see the Eucharistic bread as a substance different in kind from ordinary bread. Such an interpretation, however, misconstrues both the context and the force of Paul's warning. "Not discerning the body" refers rather to the inability of believers to grasp what it means for them to be the one body of Christ, able then to partake meaningfully in the one Eucharistic body. Their divisions and their refusal to share make the celebration of the Lord's Supper a lie. Only by realizing that by belonging to Christ we are "members of one another" (Rom 12:5) and form one body, are we able to understand correctly how the Eucharist nourishes our new life, which is in its very essence an existence with and for others. Receiving the Eucharistic bread roots us more deeply in that one body—crucified, risen from the dead and continuing its existence on earth in the women and men animated by God's Spirit, which is the same Spirit that animated Jesus.

"Discerning the body" can thus be considered the root and heart of Christian ethics, because it means passing from an individualistic outlook to a relational view of the world. In order to grasp all the consequences of this maxim, however, a further step is necessary. It begins with Jesus's distinction between "loving those who love us" and "loving our enemies" (cf. Matt 5:43–48; Luke 6:27–36). As we saw earlier in this book in our critique of triumphalism, the message of Jesus is radically opposed to the eternal human tendency to separate people into an "in-group" and an "out-group"—the good and the wicked, those who are on our side and those who are hostile or indifferent. The community of Christ's followers can never become a closed group of the elect standing over against the *massa damnata*, the multitudes who are condemned; it is the New Jerusalem with its twelve gates open all the time (cf. Rev 21:25), with walls that give it shape, but exclude no one.

On one level, it is true that someone who discovers God's love in Christ and responds to this love crosses over from "the fleshly body of death" as a member of Adam to "the spiritual body of glory" as a member of Christ (cf. 1 Cor 15:42–50). But once this transition has taken place and we are "in Christ," we realize that even before Adam, there was the Christ in whom all things were created, and in communion with him we discover our original body and receive our true name (cf. Rev 2:17). "I am the Alpha and the Omega, the First and the Last, the Beginning and the End," says the Christ of the Apocalypse (Rev 22:13). Similarly, the Letter to the Colossians tells us that God's Son is "the firstborn of all creation" in whom, through whom, and for whom all things were created, and who is likewise, as "the firstborn from the dead," the head of the body, the Church (Col 1:15–18). The body of the Risen Christ is thus not an afterthought on God's part, a shelter for a group of survivors rescued from an inhospitable environment doomed to destruction, but rather the full revelation, the *pleroma*, of humanity and all creation, a source of unfading light that extends to the furthest reaches of the universe. Christ's mission is "to bring together all things in heaven and on earth with Christ as head" (Eph 1:10), "to reconcile to himself all things" (Col 1:20). As Brother Roger of Taizé liked to say, "In the heart of God, the church is as vast as all humanity," coextensive with creation restored and renewed in Christ.

Discerning the body, then, means leaving behind the illusions of individualism and partisanship to discover our oneness in Christ—first of all with other believers, and then with the entire human family and indeed with all that exists. This does not, however, imply some sort of nebulous "oceanic feeling," which remains on the level of a disembodied contemplation. On the contrary, the unity in question is bodily and thus infallibly concrete; it is literally the most concrete of all realities that exist.[7] This communion begins with my sister or brother in faith who stands next to me, and widens to include the poor man on the corner, the family of migrants requiring assistance, and from there extends to all, especially the victims of exclusion and oppression, past, present, and future, across the world. It turns the other into someone who has a claim upon me, someone who is part of who I am and who I must therefore listen to and take seriously. It involves care for all creatures and for the material universe as well, as Pope Francis reminds us in his encyclical *Laudato Si'*. Discerning the body means, in short, realizing that I can never find fulfillment by myself, but that the input and presence of all are required for the church—and humanity—to achieve its final form. It means allowing Christ's work of universal reconciliation to take flesh in my own life. The process of *metanoia* opens up the full meaning of Jesus's words to "love our neighbor as ourselves" (Matt 22:39; Lev 19:18) and to "do unto others as we would have them do unto us" (Matt 7:12). We come gradually to see these statements not as strenuous and arbitrary acts of the will, but as simple consequences of the realization that we all form one body in Christ, a body in the end coextensive with the entire creation, with "God all in all" (1 Cor 15:28).

7. This concreteness is shown graphically by the fact that, in writing to the Christians of Corinth, Paul tells them that by having sexual relations with a prostitute they make her implicitly part of Christ's body. He places "members of Christ" (by faith and baptism) and "members of a prostitute" (by sexual intercourse) in parallel. See 1 Corinthians 6:15–17.

CONCLUSION

Standing on Our Own Feet

A few hours before his sudden and unexpected death, the
American Trappist monk Thomas Merton gave a talk to some
monks and nuns in Thailand. He spoke of the Tibetan Buddhist
monks who had left their country as the Chinese Communists
were arriving, and recalled a conversation with a friend of his, the
lama Chogyam Trungpa Rimpoche:

> When he was faced with the decision of leaving his coun-
> try, he did not quite know what to do. He was absent from
> his monastery on a visitation to some other monastery,
> and he was caught out in the mountains somewhere and
> was living in a peasant's house, wondering what to do
> next. He sent a message to a nearby abbot friend of his,
> saying; "What do we do?" The abbot sent back a strange
> message, which I think is very significant: "From now on,
> Brother, everybody stands on his own feet."[1]

And Merton commented that this was an extremely important statement, not just for Buddhists, but for Christians as well.
The monk's somewhat enigmatic reply certainly does not imply
that we are called to become individualists, nor that we must strive
to earn our own salvation by ourselves. It means rather

1. Merton, *Asian Journal*, 338.

68

> that we can no longer rely on being supported by struc-
> tures that may be destroyed at any moment. . . . You can-
> not rely on structures. The time for relying on structures
> has disappeared. They are good and they should help us,
> and we should do the best we can with them. But they
> may be taken away, and if everything is taken away, what
> do you do next?[2]

Beginning in the fourth century of our era, the Christian church in the West lost its marginal status and entered into the mainstream of a particular civilization, the Roman Empire. Like all vast historical changes, this shift took place without the actors being fully aware of what was happening, and still less of what its long-term consequences would be. This partnership between a community of faith and a human society with its political, eco-nomic and cultural institutions deeply affected both parties. On the one hand, it allowed the message of Jesus Christ to reach much of the world, like a beneficial virus carried by an unwitting host. The simile is not completely accurate, for the virus of the gospel also altered in many ways the priorities and values of the mainstream society. This cohabitation reached its apogee in the Middle Ages in what is commonly called Christendom, with periods of harmony and times of tension, as in the history of any couple. At a certain point, however, the synthesis between throne and altar began to break down, a breakdown which has taken centuries and is not yet over. Many fragments of the old worldview are still operative in certain places, and others have survived as caricatures. Still, no one really knows yet whether an unambiguously post-Christian society is possible, or what it would look like.

It can be argued, however, that at least in the more prosper-ous countries of the Western world we have reached some kind of tipping-point. And it is here that Thomas Merton's question be-comes particularly relevant: "If everything is taken away, what do you do next?" It is highly likely that the days of being nominally Christian as citizens of a particular land and of allowing the reli-gious structures of the tribe to make our decisions for us are more

2. Merton, *Asian Journal*, 338.

and more a thing of the past. Naturally, living the Christian life will always involve being part of a community of faith, and in times to come this will perhaps be truer than ever before. But in our day, at a time of great cultural upheaval, unless each believer makes a conscious choice to follow Christ and to discover what this means concretely in his or her day-to-day life, unless each person puts their trust in Christ and enters resolutely upon the path of discipleship, the faith will no longer find any points of anchorage in our human world. It will be increasingly more difficult to rely on institutions to do our believing for us, and this is the reason I have tried to indicate, in this book, what the basic shape of the Christian life should be. In my opinion it has become essential to see faith as a reality rooted in the heart of each person and leading him or her to join others in the constant process of discernment, renewal, and deepening that I have called *metanoia*.

Given this present state of affairs, it is now time to conclude by attempting to recall and develop briefly some of the fundamental insights that have arisen in the course of these reflections.

First of all, let us remember that *metanoia* is not repentance. Far from being rooted in regret over past failures and mistakes, it begins when a window opens, however briefly, on another level of reality and gives us a glimpse of something different and unexpected. This glimpse may be motivated from without, by means of new experiences that call into question an individual's habitual outlook. It may likewise come from within, sparked by a deep dissatisfaction with the life one has been living up to that point. Whatever its origin may be, at a certain moment the new reality perceived is brought into contact with the person and message of Jesus the Messiah. It is then understood as a *call*, a summons to allow that person and message to become a priority in one's existence and to transform radically one's way of relating to the world and acting in consequence. The call may be experienced as a sudden and unexpected event or, alternatively, as the fruit of a long process of searching and questioning, and the response may be immediate or hesitant. In any case, one has now turned a page and things will never be the same again.

Subsequently, a person may indeed be sorry for their past behavior and deeply regret the time wasted in what now appears as
frivolity, aimlessness, self-indulgence, or even wrongdoing. Such
an awareness certainly contributes to the ardor with which someone lives his or her new life. As time passes, however, this attitude
of remorse, which still remains to a certain extent self-centered,
will tend to deepen and broaden into a more universal sorrow for
all the ways in which humanity remains blind and deaf to its true
happiness, and unwilling to take the steps needed to remedy the
situation. This sorrow is a kind of echo of Jesus's own act of taking
upon himself all the sins of humankind.[3]

Discovering this other reality means simultaneously uncov-
ering a deeper part of oneself. The process of *metanoia* involves
"heading out into deep water" (Luke 5:4). In the parlance of today,
we could say that in addition to giving someone a new conscious
understanding of existence, it penetrates and modifies the unconscious mind. For this reason it is fundamentally different from
receiving information or putting explicit directives into practice;
it cannot be limited to a catechesis consisting in "truths" to be
assented to intellectually. Here once again we come upon Saint
Paul's distinction between law and Spirit. *Metanoia* means allowing God's Spirit to take hold of our inner life and transform the
roots of our being, which are no longer closed upon themselves
but now open to the workings of grace. As a new way of viewing
reality takes shape and new insights arise in our minds, these can
and indeed must be articulated, but their source lies beyond our
understanding. The impulse for our acts comes from what Saint
Paul calls "the inner being" (Eph 3:16; 2 Cor 4:16) and Jesus "the
heart" (Matt 12:34; 15:18–19; Mark 7:21; Luke 6:45; cf. John 7:38).
No list of instructions, no program or algorithm can fully define or
direct the life of those who surrender themselves to the workings
of the Holy Spirit.

3. See John of Taizé, *Wrath*, where I described this sorrow at humanity's
refusal to live authentically as the deepest meaning of the topic of "God's anger" in the Bible.

From what has already been said, it should be clear that *metanoia* cannot be a one-time conversion event but is rather a lifelong process. More exactly, *metanoia* is the life itself of a follower of Christ. To employ a human image, it means not just "falling in love" but, more importantly, "being in love."[4] In a phrase from the fourth-century bishop and theologian Gregory of Nyssa dear to the founder of Taizé, *metanoia* leads us "from one beginning to another, through beginnings which have no end."[5] The "beginning," recapitulated in the sacrament of baptism, involves leaving behind one's old ways to enter into the new life of a disciple. But this new life can never be possessed in tranquility; once we think we have arrived, we have already abandoned the way of the Lord for our own human schemes and fabrications. Believers are called to live as "strangers and sojourners" in the midst of their fellows (1 Pet 2:11); symbolically, like Abraham and Sara, they dwell in tents even in the promised land (cf. Heb 11:8–10), ready when necessary to break camp and set out on the road once again. Their homelessness may at times be a cause of distress, and is only endurable because they have found a new home in God.

The Christian life is thus essentially a life on the move. It loses its vitality when life becomes too easy, when we remain stuck in our comfort zones. This is one of the reasons why, in Scripture, trials and tribulations are so often associated with the life of faith.[6] Not out of some perverse love of suffering, though it must be admitted that this has at times been a temptation in Christian preaching and spirituality, but essentially because the difficulties of the journey keep us from settling down and require us to turn to God, open to an unexpected dynamism into which we can only enter each day anew.

4. The Canadian Jesuit theologian Bernard Lonergan (1904–84) described religious conversion as "falling in love with God" and the life of grace as "an unrestricted being in love." See for example his *Method in Theology*, 122–23, 240–41.

5. Gregory of Nyssa, *Hom. in Cant.* 8, *PG* 44, 941C.

6. "[Paul and Barnabas] fortified the souls of the disciples, encouraging them to persevere in the faith, and telling them 'we have to pass through many trials in order to enter the Kingdom of God'" (Acts 14:22).

In the final analysis, being a follower of Jesus means living fully in God's today. One of the consequences of *metanoia* is therefore gradually to uproot us from a fixation on things past and future. Nostalgia for a world long gone, as well as clinging to yesterday's hurts on the one hand, and obsession with dreams or fears for the future on the other, take us out of the present and make us unfit for the kingdom of God, which only comes to us in the here and now. God is the Eternal Now, in the words of Paul Tillich quoted earlier, and the fulfillment of all our longings is nothing other than the Real Presence of the divine. Unfortunately it is not God who is absent but we, living habitually as we do in an unfocused manner that distracts and disperses us. Were we able to be fully present, we would discover that all we have been frantically searching for elsewhere lies right in front of us, closer to us than we are to ourselves.

Humanly speaking, it may seem contradictory to speak both of a life on the move and one that is rooted in the present. The solution to this antinomy comes from a deeper awareness of the unique quality of the divine Now. It is not a static reality, one that can be possessed either at present or in an age to come. It continually eludes our grasp and, in so doing, sets us on the road.[7] In the Gospels, this stands out most clearly in the encounters with the risen Christ. As soon as the two disciples realize that their companion on the road to Emmaus was in fact their crucified Master, now fully alive, "their eyes were opened and they recognized him; and he became unmanifest to them. . . . At that very hour, they rose up and returned to Jerusalem" (Luke 24:31–33). It should be noted that the text does not say that Jesus left them and went away elsewhere, to some faraway heaven. Although he is no longer accessible to their senses, he sets them on the road back to the community, where they discover that others have had an identical experience. In effect, the Risen Lord is still at work reconfiguring

---

7. Cf. the theme chosen by Brother Alois of Taizé for his "Proposals 2020" to the young people, based on an expression describing the life of Urszula Ledochowska, the founder of the Ursuline sisters of Poland: "Always on the move, never uprooted."

his body and animating it with his Spirit, along the lines of the prophet Ezekiel's famous vision of the dry bones (see Ezek 37).

Metanoia thus sets us on the road with Christ. During his years on earth, Jesus "had no place to lay his head" (Matt 8:20). He "went about doing good" (Acts 10:38), and finally out of faithfulness to his Abba went up to Jerusalem, where rejection and a horrifying and shameful death awaited him, offering him the unique opportunity to testify to the stupefying depths of divine love and forgiveness. As his followers, freed of any need to justify or create meaning for ourselves, we are similarly enabled to go towards the broken places of humanity and witness there to a healing and reconciling Presence.

In the Bible the desert or wilderness is, by definition, the region where no one can settle down; it is a place through which one passes. Paradoxically, in the steps of Christ Jesus, recapitulated in his journey from Good Friday to Easter Sunday, Christians make their home in this wasteland (cf. Rev 12:6, 14), where they belong to no one but to God. At the same time, because they belong to God alone and are part of the universal body of his Christ, they are linked to everyone. Henceforth nothing or nobody is alien to them. Between his death and his resurrection, on Holy Saturday, Jesus filled the universe with his life-giving presence (cf. Eph 4:7–10). Our existence as Christians takes place in the Holy Saturday of history,[8] and we are able to live in this no man's land solely because we have found our true rest in Christ.

Finally, the change of heart which is called *metanoia* transforms both our understanding and our actions. It is a movement "from shadows and appearances to reality."[9] Little by little it strips us of the illusions that keep us from being fully present to the people and events around us, providing a wisdom that often takes the form of an "unknowing," a deeper recognition of our inner poverty. It does this not by starting from the results of rational argument but by modifying the basic postulates that determine how

8. See John of Taizé, *Life on the Edge*, Part IV.

9. *Ex umbris et imaginibus ad veritatem.* This was the epitaph chosen by John Henry Newman (1801–1890) for his tomb, to sum up his life's journey.

we see the world. Some of these are so fallacious that they lead to harmful and even self-destructive choices and behavior, and yet they usually lie beneath the threshold of consciousness, and so are very resistant to change. That is why only a "divine therapy," namely the inner working of God's Spirit, can accomplish this task. Otherwise we risk changing our explicit beliefs but leaving intact the underlying postulates; our conversion remains merely notional, and so cannot be life-giving.

This changed understanding inevitably leads to a change in behavior. Here too, it is primarily a matter of giving God room to act. Living as an active part of Christ's body on earth means that Christ can continue to be present through us. Saint Paul expressed this in a particularly dramatic way when he wrote to the believers in Galatia: "I have been crucified with Christ and it is not I who live any longer: Christ lives in me" (Gal 2:19–20). To use another Pauline turn of phrase, we could say that if we are in Christ, then Christ is in us.

But how can God's own Son be present and active in our banal and imperfect human lives? In the Sermon on the Mount, Jesus characterizes his followers by two powerful images that recapitulate the grammar of Christian acting:

> You are the salt of the earth. But if salt loses its saltiness, how can it be effective? It is good for nothing but to be thrown out and trampled underfoot. You are the light of the world. A city set on a hill cannot be hidden. Nor does anyone light a lamp and put it under a basket; they put it on the lampstand, so it can give light to all those in the house. In the same way, let your light shine out, so that people may see your good deeds and give glory to your heavenly Father. (Matt 5:13–16)

It is significant that here Jesus does not give advice on how to behave, on what to do in specific situations. Instead, he points out two potential pitfalls that hinder God from working through us. The first is "to lose our saltiness." Whether this refers to salt as a seasoning or, more probably, to a substance used to light a fire or keep it burning, especially in connection with offering sacrifices to God, the meaning is clear. The ability to act authentically, to be people who bring the Beatitudes to life, does not come from us, but from our relationship to Christ. If we allow that relationship to deteriorate, then our activity will be fruitless, however efficient it is in human terms. The primary question then is not "What should we do?" but "How can we keep alive our bond with Christ and so remain a living member of his body?" Here, prayer is of the utmost importance, as well as meditation on God's word in Scripture and participation in the life of a faith-community. If we remain attached to the vine (cf. John 15), Jesus tells us, the rest will follow.

The second threat to Christian living is "to put our light under a basket." This certainly cannot mean publicizing or drawing attention to our purportedly selfless acts; that would only be imitating the error of those play-actors who put on a religious show in order to be seen by others (Matt 6:1–6; cf. 23:5–7). The "basket" here that hides what is essential is more likely all those human considerations—fears and prejudices, the need for acceptance, conformity, tortuous reasoning—which complicate what is simple, which keep the clear light of the gospel from shining out in our lives. When this light enters us, gradually it burns away these hindrances that prevent it from being seen in all its radiance. This is of course the work of an entire lifetime, but it has already begun when a person hears the call "Come, follow me" and attempts to respond in his or her human frailty. Such people are already signs of a different reality, far more than they may ever realize. To be on the road with Christ Jesus is already, in some sense, to have arrived, since he is the one who "initiates our faith and brings it to completion" (Heb 12:2).

Bibliography

Agamben, Giorgio. *The Mystery of Evil: Benedict XVI and the End of Days.* Stanford: Stanford University Press, 2017.

Augustine. *St. Augustine's Confessions: With an English Translation.* Translated by William Watts. Edited by W. H. D. Rouse. 2 vols. Loeb Classical Library 26–27. London: Heinemann, 1950. https://archive.org/details/staugustinesconfo1augu/page/8/mode/2up.

Day, Dorothy. *The Long Loneliness.* New York: HarperCollins, 2009.

Delumeau, Jean. *La Peur en Occident (xive–xviiie siècles): Une cité assiégée.* Paris: Fayard, 1978.

———. *Sin and Fear: The Emergence of a Western Guilt Culture, 13th–18th Centuries.* New York: St. Martin's, 1991.

Deneen, Patrick. *Why Liberalism Failed.* New Haven, CT: Yale University Press, 2018.

Ellul, Jacques. *The Subversion of Christianity.* Translated by Geoffrey W. Bromiley. Eugene, OR: Wipf & Stock, 2011.

Francis, Pope. *Laudato Si'.* http://w2.vatican.va/content/francesco/en/encyclicals/documents/papa-francesco_20150524_enciclica-laudato-si.html.

John of Taizé, Brother. *Life on the Edge: Holy Saturday and the Recovery of the End Time.* Eugene, OR: Cascade, 2017.

———. *The Wrath of a Loving God: Unraveling a Biblical Conundrum.* Eugene, OR: Cascade, 2019.

John Paul II, Pope. *Redemptor hominis.* http://www.vatican.va/content/john-paul-ii/en/encyclicals/documents/hf_jp-ii_enc_04031979_redemptor-hominis.html.

Johnson, Luke Timothy. *Among the Gentiles: Greco-Roman Religion and Christianity.* New Haven, CT: Yale University Press, 2009.

Kegan, Robert. *The Evolving Self: Problem and Process in Human Development.* 2nd ed. Cambridge, MA: Harvard University Press, 1982.

Landrivon, S. "L'Écriture mythologisée: de la Madeleine à *La Traviata*, histoire d'une dérive." *Nouvelle Revue Théologique* 141 (2019) 177–88.

Bibliography

Langer, Suzanne. *Philosophy in a New Key: A Study in the Symbolism of Reason, Rite, and Art.* 1957. Reprint, Cambridge, MA: Harvard University Press, 1996.

Lewis, C. S. *Surprised by Joy.* New York: Harper Collins, 2017.

Lonergan, Bernard. *Method in Theology.* Toronto: University of Toronto Press, 1971.

Marable, Manning. *Malcolm X: A Life of Reinvention.* New York: Penguin, 2011.

Merton, Thomas. *The Asian Journal of Thomas Merton.* New York: New Directions, 1975.

———. *The Seven Storey Mountain.* New York: Harcourt, 1999.

Newman, John Henry. *An Essay on the Development of Christian Doctrine.* 1845. Reprint, Westminster, MD: Christian Classics, 1968.

Pascal, Blaise. *Pensées and Other Writings.* Translated by Honor Levi. Oxford World's Classics. Oxford: Oxford University Press, 1995.

Percy, Walker. *The Message in the Bottle.* New York: Farrar, Straus & Giroux, 1975.

Rilke, Rainer Maria. *Duinser Elegien.* Leipzig: Insel Verlag, 1923.

Robinson, John A. T. *The Body: A Study in Pauline Theology.* London: SCM, 1952.

Roger of Taizé, Brother. *The Rule of Taizé.* London: SPCK, 2012.

———. *The Wonder of a Love.* London: Mowbray, 1981.

Simmel, Georg. "Das Abenteuer." In *Philosophische Kultur: Gesammelte Essays,* 7–24. 2nd ed. Leipzig: Kroner, 1919. English translation: http://condor.depaul.edu/dweinste/theory/adventure.html.

Tertullian. *Adversus Marcionem.* Edited and translated by Ernest Evans. Oxford: Oxford University Press, 1972. http://www.tertullian.org/articles/evans_marc/evans_marc_00index.htm.

Paul VI, Pope. *Gaudium et Spes: Pastoral Constitution on the Church in the Modern World.* http://www.vatican.va/archive/hist_councils/ii_vatican_council/documents/vat-ii_const_19651207_gaudium-et-spes_en.html.

Walden, Treadwell. *The Great Meaning of Metanoia: An Undeveloped Chapter in the Life and Teaching of Christ.* Rev. ed. New York: Whittaker, 1896. https://archive.org/details/greatmeaningofmeoowaldiala.

X, Malcolm, and Alex Haley. *The Autobiography of Malcolm X.* New York: Ballantine, 2015.

Scripture Index

Scripture Index